# 2's Felt Board Fun EXPERIENCE

by
**Liz & Dick Wilmes**

Illustrations by
**Janet McDonnell**

A  Publication

38W567 Brindlewood, Elgin, Illinois   60123

# ART
## Cover Design and Graphics:

David VanDelinder

STUDIO 155

Elgin, Illinois 60123

## Computer Graphics:

David Jensen

Greg Wilmes

Elgin, IL 60120

## Text/Pattern Graphics:

Janet McDonnell

Early Childhood Artist

Arlington Heights, Illinois  60004

## SPECIAL THANKS TO:

Cheryl Luppino and Mary Steinman for sharing many of the fingerplays and games they play with their toddlers and twos along with the techniques they use to make each one appropriate, fun, and exciting.

## PUBLISHED BY:

38W567 BRINDLEWOOD

ELGIN, ILLINOIS 60123

ISBN 0-943452-19-8

Dedicated to teachers
who make stories, rhymes
and activities come alive for
their very young children.

# CONTENTS

# FELT BOARD HINTS

**When doing felt board activities with very young children,**

## REMEMBER TO:

### PRACTICE BEFORE DOING THEM

• Have STORY and ACTIVITY CARDS to help you remember the sequence of each idea.

• Use voice inflections for the different characters.

• Tell Stories at an appropriate pace, too slow or fast and the children loose interest.

• Move the pieces around the board to give the activity or story even more action.

### BE PREPARED

• Know the activities you're going to do.

• Have all of your felt pieces and props within easy reach.

• Have the felt pieces and props in order.

### GET THE CHILDREN'S ATTENTION AS THEY GATHER

• Sing a related song or do a fingerplay.

• Set up the felt board and talk about the pieces with the children as they come together.

### PICK CHILDREN'S FAVORITE ACTIVITIES

• Have them readily available.

• Do them often. Young children "love" repetition.

### KEEP FELT PIECES HIDDEN UNTIL
### THEY GO UP ON THE BOARD

• Tuck them under your leg.

• Set them behind the felt board.

• Keep them in an envelop.

### HAVE AS FEW PIECES AS POSSIBLE ON THE BOARD AT THE SAME TIME

• Put the pieces on the board one at a time.

• Take each piece off the board as soon as you have finished with it.

# MAKE YOUR FELT BOARD PIECES

**HINT:** Make pieces which you use only for the activities. Make other pieces which the children use when they do activities on their own.

**PIECES FOR YOUR FELT BOARDS CAN BE MADE IN DIFFERENT WAYS. CHOOSE THE BEST ONE FOR THE ACTIVITY YOU ARE DOING.**

## FELT PIECES

1. Transfer the pattern onto the felt. You can do this several ways:
   - Duplicate the pattern. Cut it out. Outline the pattern on the felt.
   - Trace the pattern from the book onto a sheet of tissue paper, pin the pattern on the felt.
   - Use a tracing wheel and dressmaker's carbon. Lay the felt and carbon paper under the pattern in the book. Using a tracing wheel, trace the pattern onto the felt you've chosen.

2. Cut out the main pattern piece. Add details by gluing smaller pieces of felt to the main piece or drawing the details with permanent, non-toxic markers.

3. Keep your pieces flat by periodically ironing them.

## PELLON PIECES

1. Lay heavyweight pellon on top of the pattern.

2. Trace the pattern right onto the pellon.

3. Color the pattern with embroidery ink, non-toxic markers, or crayons.

## PAPER PIECES

1. Duplicate the pattern.

2. Color the picture.

3. Cut it out.

4. Back it with a large piece of felt.

# MAKE YOUR

## THERE ARE MANY SIZES AND STYLES OF FELT BOARDS.

### BASIC BOARDS

Get a heavy piece of cardboard or thin plywood. Wrap a piece of felt around it and tape or 'hot-glue' the felt to the back of the board. Construct this type of board in various sizes — lap board about 1 foot square for individual work; a medium size board about 1 1/2 feet by 2 feet for small group work; and a large board for full-group activities.

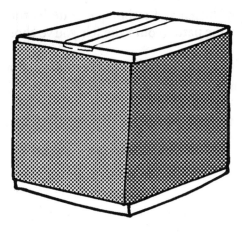

### FOUR-IN-ONE BOARDS

Get a large, sturdy cardboard box from the grocery store. Tape the top and bottom closed. Cover the four remaining sides of the box with felt. Great for individual or several children.

### PORTABLE FELT BOARDS

Using the instructions for the *Basic Board*, make a board approximately 12"x14." Staple a loop of cord to the top of the board, so you can wear it around your neck. Choose a felt activity which your children like. As you are talking with the children during free choice, do the activity as often as the children would like.

# FELT BOARDS

## Some you can purchase and others you can make.

### FELT FOLDERS

Cut an 11"x14" piece of posterboard. Fold it in half (11"x81/2"). Reinforce the fold with a piece of duct tape. Fold it again to get a good crease. Open the posterboard and cover it with a piece of felt. With this type of board, leave a little slack in the felt so that it will easily open and close.

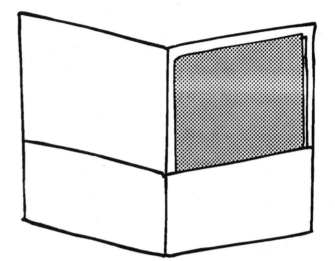

Lay the felt pieces you want the children to use on one side of the board, close it, and put the felt board in a pocket folder. On the front of the folder draw a very simple picture to indicate what felt board activity is in the folder. For example, you might draw a square to indicate a shape activity. Put several felt folders on the manipulative shelf. The children can use them during free choice.

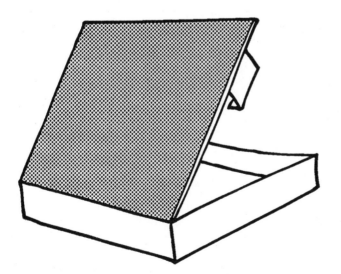

### PIZZA BOX BOARDS

Get clean pizza boxes from your local pizza restaurant. For each board cut a piece of felt the size of the lid. Glue it on the top.

Store the felt pieces in the box. Use a short, wide-diameter, dowel rod to prop the lid open and keep it at a slight angle while using the board.

# FARM ANIMALS

## MAKE

Cow
Pig
Horse
Chicken
Rooster
Duck
Sheep
Cat
Dog
Donkey
Turkey
Frog

## MAKE

All of the farm animals from the activity, GOOD MORNING, COW

## PROPS

Shoe Box

## GOOD MORNING, COW:

Have all of the farm animals behind the felt board. Put them on the board one at a time. Have everyone say, *"Good morning"* or *"Good afternoon"* to the animal depending on the time of day. For example, put a cow on the board. Everyone says, *"Good morning, Cow."* You can say, *"How would the cow say 'Good morning' to you?"* Let the children make cow noises. Put a second animal on the board and continue the game.

Slowly *"walk"* each animal off the board and put it out of sight behind the board. As each animal is leaving, make the animal's noise and have the children wave good-bye.

## GOOD NIGHT, PIG:

Just before nap time gather the children around the felt board. Shhh! Quietly and gently put one animal on the board. Have the children whisper what the animal is, such as *"Pig."* Then in a very quiet voice, say *"Good night, Pig."* Take the pig off of the board and lay it down in the shoe box. Continue, putting each farm animal to sleep.

After all of the animals are in bed, slowly tiptoe with the children to their cots and say, *"Good night"* to each of them as they lie down.

EXTENSION: After nap time gather around the felt board again. Wake up each animal. Slowly put each one on the board as if they are stretching and waking up. Say *"Hi"* to them using their voices.

# FARM ANIMALS

## MAKE

All of the farm
   animals from the
   activity, GOOD
   MORNING, COW

Large felt outline of
   a barn structure

## IN AND OUT OF THE BARN:

Put the large barn structure on the felt board. Have all of the animals in front of you.

Pick up one animal and *"walk"* it to the felt board. As you're *"walking"* the animal, encourage the children to make the animal's noises.

When you get to the felt board, ask the children if you should put the animal *"in"* or *"out"* of the barn. Put the animal where the children say. As you place it on the board say, *"The cow is _____ the barn."* Let the children call out *"in"* or *"out"* and then clap for the animal.

# FARM ANIMALS

## MAKE

All of the farm
   animals from the
   activity, GOOD
   MORNING, COW
Old McDonald
Barn

## OLD McDONALD HAD A FARM:

Put Old McDonald and the barn on the felt board. Have all of the farm animals on the floor tucked under your leg.

Begin singing OLD McDONALD HAD A FARM. As you're singing, *"And on his farm he had a ..."* put one animal on the felt board near the barn. The children name that animal as they sing, adding the animal's sounds.

As you begin singing the second verse, take the first animal away. At the appropriate time put up another animal. Continue in this manner until you've sung about all of the farm animals.

After singing, say to the children, *"Let's see all of Old McDonald's animals."* Put them up one at a time and have the children call out who they are and/or make the animal's noises.

Pretend that it is night time. Very quietly say to the children, *"Time for all of the animals to go to sleep. Good night, _____."* Continue taking them down whispering, *"Good night"* to each one.

### OLD MC DONALD

Old Mc Donald had a farm — E-I-E-I-O.
And on his farm he had a cow — E-I-E-I-O.
With a "moo-moo" here, and a "moo-moo" there,
Here a "moo", there a "moo"
Everywhere a "moo-moo"

*Continue with other animals and their sounds.*

# FARM ANIMALS

## MAKE

All of the farm
   animals from the
   activity, GOOD
   MORNING, COW

Barn with large
   doors which
   open from the
   activity, IN AND
   OUT OF THE
   BARN

## MAKE

Child
Black cat
Brown horse
Red cow
Green duck
Pink pig
Yellow dog

## PROPS

I WENT WALKING
   book or copy of
   STORY CARD

## WHO'S BEHIND THE BARN DOORS:

Put the large barn on the felt board. Hide all of the animals behind the board so the children can't see them.

Have the children cover their eyes. Hide an animal behind the barn doors. Say to the children, *"Let's see who's behind the barn doors?"* Open one door. Let the children call out the animal and make his noises. Open the other door to see the whole animal. Clap for him!!

Have the children cover their eyes again. Take the one animal away and put a new one behind the doors. Continue with all of the animals.

## I WENT WALKING, Story Card

Duplicate the STORY CARD, glue it to a piece of construction paper and laminate or cover it with clear adhesive paper.

Put the child on the left side of your felt board and the farm animals in order behind the board. *"Walk"* the child as you begin telling the story. Put the black cat behind the child. *"Walk"* the child and cat and continue telling the story. At the end of the story, all of the farm animals will be walking behind the child.

# I WENT WALKING

## by Sue Williams

The story begins with the child saying, "I went walking." An imaginary character says, "What did you see?"

The child answers, "I saw a black cat looking at me."

The story continues with the child spotting the different farm animals. They form a parade. The order of animals is

**Black cat**

**Brown horse**

**Red cow**

**Green duck**

**Pink pig**

**Yellow dog.**

The story ends with all of the animals in a parade behind the child.

# Good Morning, Cow

17

**Good Morning, Cow**

# Good Morning, Cow

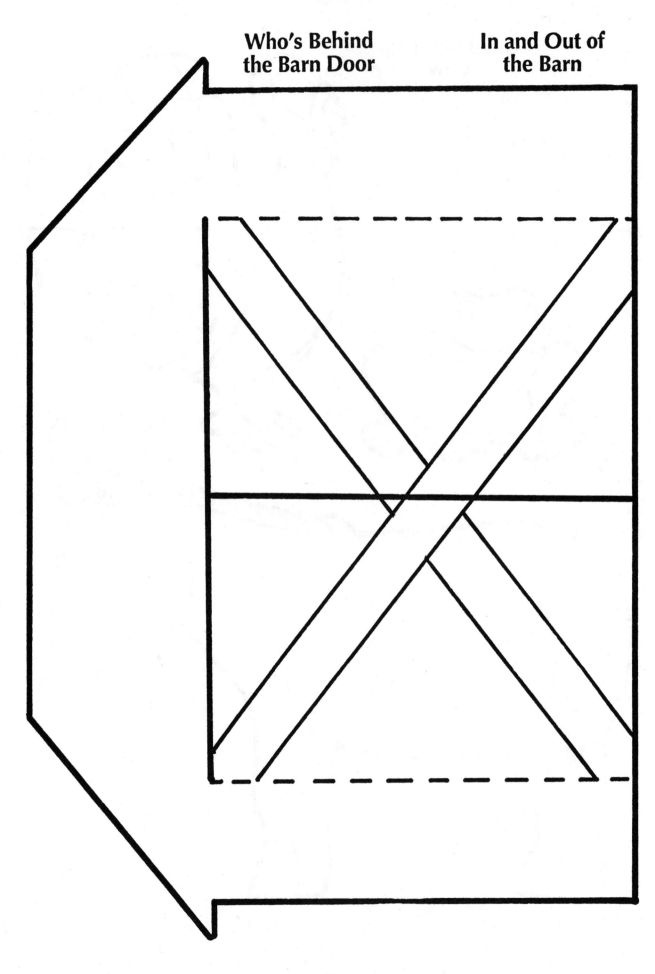

**Old McDonald Had a Farm**

**Old McDonald
Had a Farm**

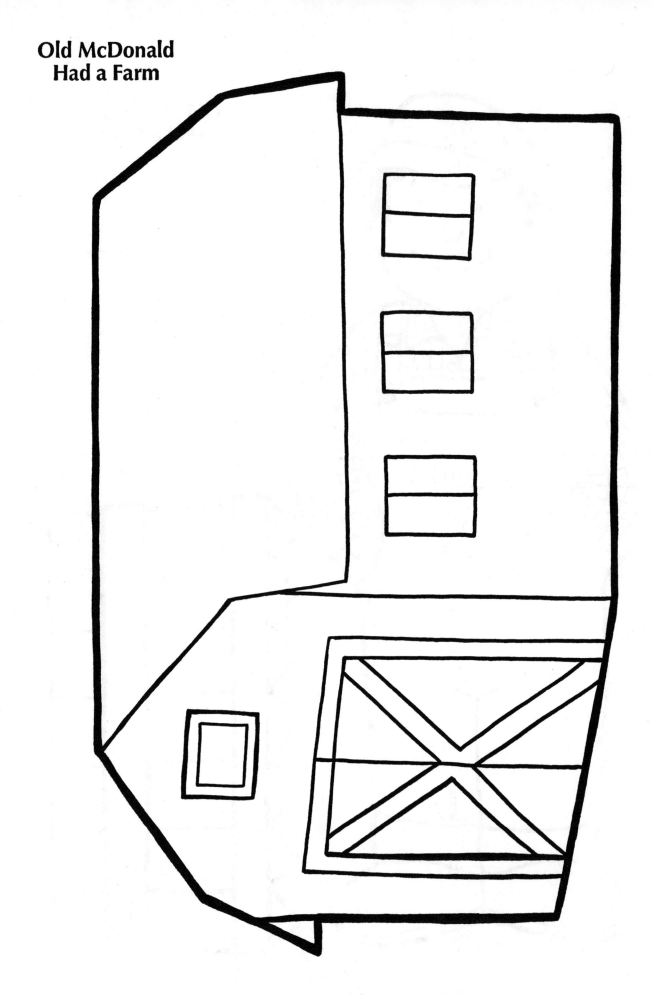

# I Went Walking

# BEARS

## MAKE

Mountain
Smaller bear

## FOR VARIATIONS:

Animals and objects
your children will
easily recognize.

## THE BEAR WENT OVER THE MOUNTAIN

Put the mountain on the felt board with the bear at the bottom of it.

Sing THE BEAR WENT OVER THE MOUNTAIN with the children. As you're singing, *"walk"* the bear up to the top of the mountain and sit him there to look around. When you sing *"...to see what he could see..."* touch something in the room that is near you — floor, table, chair, puzzle, rug, etc. Let the children call out what you're touching. *"Run"* the bear down the mountain as the children slap their thighs. Then as you *"walk"* the bear up the mountain sing again to discover what he sees next in the room.

VARIATION: Put all of the felt objects and animals behind the felt board. Instead of naming objects in the room, put a felt object or animal on the other side of the mountain. When the bear gets to the top, let the children call out what the object is.

## THE BEAR WENT OVER THE MOUNTAIN

The bear went over the mountain
The bear went over the mountain
The bear went over the mountain
To see what he could see.

*What did the bear see?*

27

# BEARS

## MAKE

Forest
Two-story house
Bed
Goldilocks
Papa bear
Mama bear
Baby bear
Bowls of porridge
Rocking chair

## THREE BEARS

As the children are gathering, put all of the pieces on the felt board so that it becomes a scene of the story. Talk with the children about the pieces as you put them up.

Using different voices tell the children a simple version of the story, GOLDILOCKS AND THE THREE BEARS. Point to the pieces and characters as you go along. After the children know the story, encourage them to use the characters' voices and say the repetitive lines with you.

EXTENSION: If appropriate, take this opportunity to talk with the children about never going with strangers or going into strangers' houses. Talk about what Goldilocks should have done.

# BEARS

# BEARS

## MAKE

House
Bridge
Pond
Tree
Cave
Bear with big eyes

## LET'S GO ON A BEAR HUNT

Put the house on the left side of your felt board and the cave with the bear hiding in it on the right side.

Say GOING ON A BEAR HUNT and do the actions with the children. When you get to the *"bridge"* put it on the board next to the house. Add each piece as you go on your *"Hunt."* As you race back home, after finding the bear, you will have your path laid out. After you've passed each marker on the path, take it off the board and replace it with the bear. At the end you'll be safely inside your home and the bear will be outside. Let the bear *"walk"* back to his home in the cave.

## GOING ON A BEAR HUNT

Let's go on a bear hunt.
All right, let's go. *(Tap your hands on your thighs like walking.)*

Open the door.
Walk down the sidewalk.
Go out to the path.

Oh look, I see a bridge.
Can't go under it.
Can't go around it.
Let's go over it. *(While sitting march feet on floor.)*

*(Continue walking and looking.)*

Oh look, I see a pond
Can't go under it.
Can't go around it.
Let's go across it. (Swim across.)

*(Continue walking and looking.)*

Oh look, I see a tree.
Can't go under it.
Can't go over it.
Let's climb up it. *(Hand over hand. Look around.)*

*(Continue walking and looking.)*

Oh look, I see a cave.
Can't go under it.
Can't go around it.
Let's go in it.

It's dark in here.
I better use my flashlight.
Doesn't work.

I think I see something.
It is big!
It is furry!
It's got a big nose!
I think it is a bear!

IT IS A BEAR!
LET'S GET OUT OF HERE!!

*(Repeat everything backwards as fast as you can until you get home.)*

31

# BEARS

## MAKE

Brown bear
Red bird
Yellow duck
Blue horse
Green frog
Purple cat
White dog
Black sheep
Goldfish
Teacher
Group of children

## PROPS

BROWN BEAR
   book or
copy of STORY
   CARD

## BROWN BEAR, BROWN BEAR, Story Card

Duplicate the STORY CARD, glue it to a piece of construction paper and laminate or cover it with clear adhesive paper

Put *"Brown Bear"* on your felt board and the other animals in order behind the board. Tell the children the BROWN BEAR, BROWN BEAR, WHAT DO YOU SEE? story in a variety of ways.

• FELT STORY: The first several times you tell the story to the children, put the pieces on the board as you tell it. (This will help the children quickly learn the sequence.) Encourage the children to say the story with you as they learn the rhythm of the lines. At the end of the story, when goldfish sees the beautiful children, point to and name all of your children. Clap for everyone.

• ANIMAL SOUNDS: Put *"Brown Bear"* on the board. Say, *"Brown bear, brown bear who do you see? I see _____."* (Let the children make the sound of the animal [redbird] who Brown Bear sees. As they are making bird sounds put the redbird on the felt board.) Continue making animal sounds throughout the story.

• PEEK-A-BOO: Put *"Brown Bear"* on the felt board. Have the children cover their eyes. Say, *"Brown bear, brown bear who do you see?"* Put the redbird on the board, have the children uncover their eyes and say, *"I see redbird looking at me."* (The children cover their eyes again.) You say the next line, *"Red bird, red bird who do you see?"* The children uncover their eyes and say, *"I see yellow duck looking at me."* Continue in this manner until you've peeked at all of the animals.

# BEARS

• ADD RHYMES TO THE STORY:
As you name each animal or make its sound or after
you've told the whole story, say a rhyme about
the animal/s with the children.

## TWO LITTLE REDBIRDS

Two little redbirds *(Fists behind back.)*
Sitting on the hill.
One named Jack *(One thumb out front.)*
And one named Jill. *(Other thumb out front.)*

Fly away Jack. *(First fist behind back.)*
Fly away Jill. *(Other fist behind back.)*
Come back Jack. *(First fist out front.)*
Come back Jill. *(Other fist out front.)*

## GUNK, GUNK

Gunk, gunk went
The little green frog one day. *(Flick hands near eyes.)*
Gunk, gunk went
The little green frog. *(Flick hands near eyes.)*

Gunk, gunk went
The little green frog one day. *(Flick hands near eyes.)*
And his eyes went
Blink, blink, blink. *(Open and shut eyes.)*

## SOFT KITTY

Soft kitty, warm kitty. *(Make a fist.)*
Little ball of fur. *(Pet the kitty.)*

Lazy kitty, pretty kitty
Purr, purr, purr. *(Whisper.)*

# BEARS

### THE PUPPY

Call the puppy.
And give him some milk.
Brush his coat
Till it shines like silk.

Call the dog
And give him a bone.
Take him for a walk,
Then put him in his home.


### BAA, BAA BLACK SHEEP

Baa, baa black sheep
Have you any wool?
Yes, sir. Yes, sir.
Three bags full.

One for my master.
One for my dame.
One for the little boy
Who lives down the lane.


### THE FISH

I hold my fingers like a fish, *(Put hands together.)*
And wave them as I go. *(Go back and forth.)*

See them swimming with a swish,
So swiftly to and fro. *(Swim quickly.*
  *Make fish lips by puckering your lips and making*
  *kissing sounds.)*

# BEARS

### FIVE LITTLE DUCKS

Five little ducks
That I once knew *(Put hand in air.)*
Fat ones, skinny ones
Tall ones too.

But the one little duck with the
Feather on his back *(Wave hand behind back.)*
He led the others with a
*"Quack, quack, quack."*


### GITTY-UP

Gitty-up, gitty-up, gitty-up
Up — up! *(Move thighs in rhythm to the song.)*

Gitty-up, gitty-up, gitty-up
Up — up!

Gitty-up, gitty-up, gitty-up
Up — up!

Whoooooa ————— Horsey *(Raise arms high in air.)*

# BEAR BEAR, BROWN BEAR, WHAT DO YOU SEE?

## by Bill Martin

The story begins "Brown Bear, Brown Bear, What do you see?"

Brown Bear answers, "I see redbird looking at me."

The story continues with each animal spotting the next one in the series.

The characters in order are:

**Brown Bear**
**Redbird**
**Yellow Duck**
**Blue Horse**
**Green Frog**
**Purple Cat**
**White Dog**
**Black Sheep**
**Goldfish**
**Mother**
**Group of Children**

**The Bear Went
Over the
Mountain**

**Three Bears**

**Three Bears**

# Three Bears

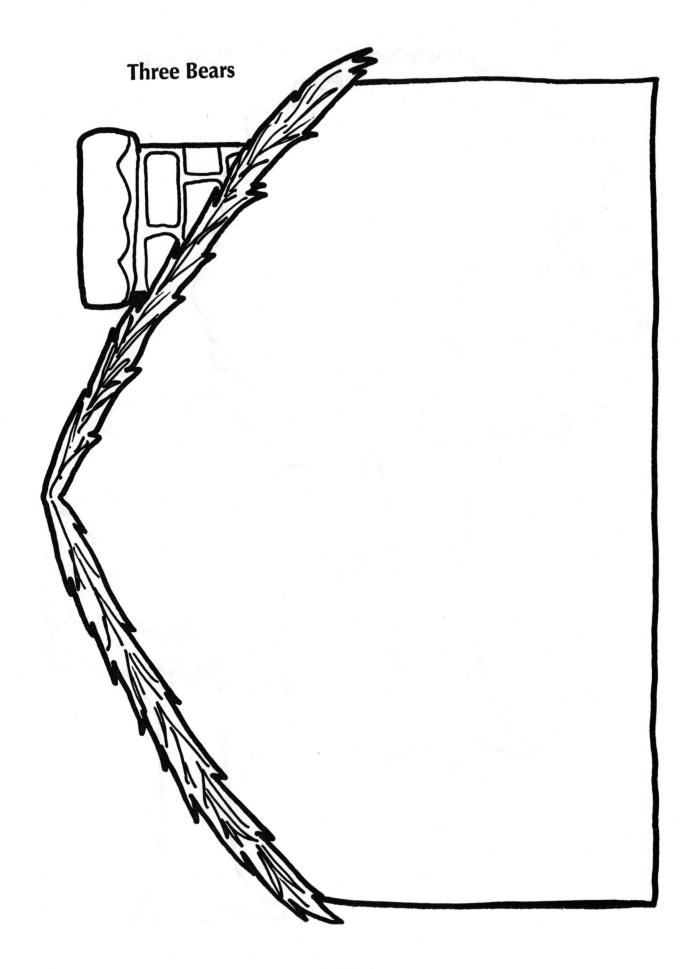

# Three Bears

## Three Bears

# Three Bears

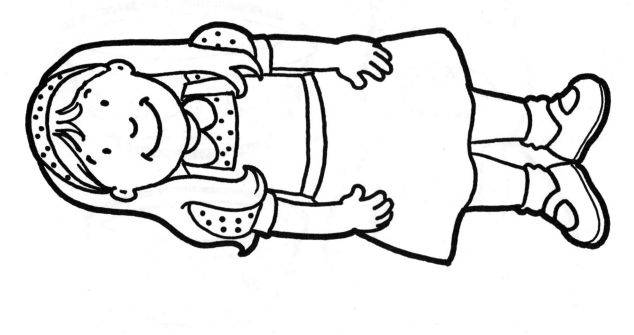

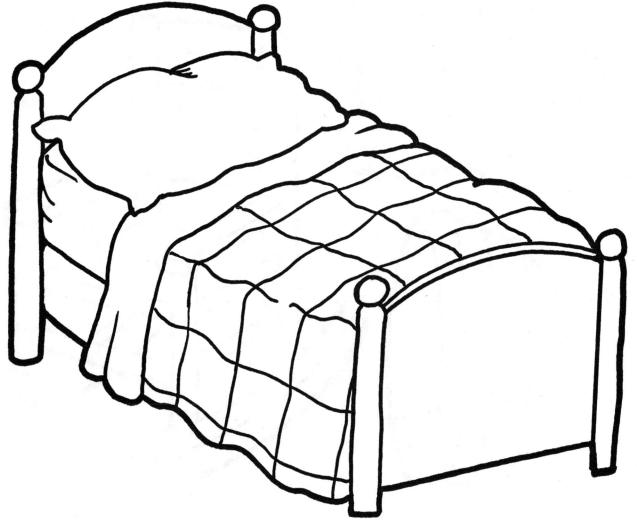

47

**Let's Go On a
Bear Hunt**

Brown Bear,
Brown Bear

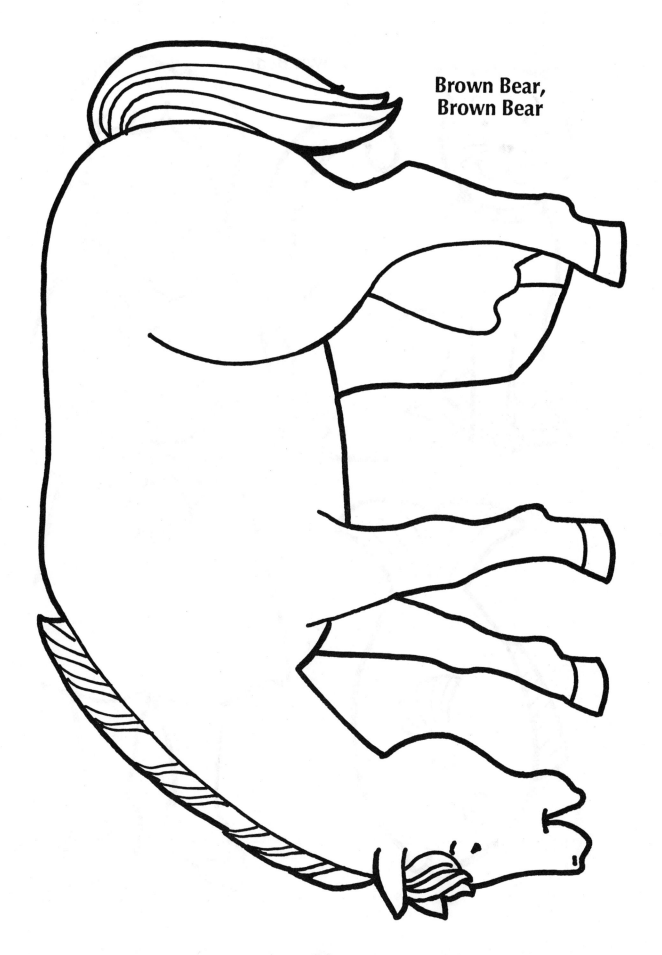

Brown Bear,
Brown Bear

**Brown Bear, Brown Bear**

Brown Bear,
Brown Bear

# Brown Bear,
# Brown Bear

# MORE ANIMALS

## MAKE

2 large trees
5 monkeys
Alligator
(or use puppet)

## PROPS

Alligator puppet
(Sock would be
great.)

## FIVE LITTLE MONKEYS SWINGING FROM THE TREE

Put both trees on the felt board. Place the 5 monkeys in one of the trees. As you do count them aloud. (The children who want will count along with you.) Have the alligator hiding under your leg.

Start saying the fingerplay. As you do bring the alligator out and have him swim slowly and quietly towards the playful monkeys. Let him *snap* at one of the monkeys. Quickly jump the monkey to the other tree so that she lands behind the second tree — peeking out to watch what happens. Continue with the rhyme until all five monkeys have narrowly escaped.

Say to the children, *"What happened to all of the monkeys?"* (Talk.) *"Let's see if they are sitting in the other tree."* (Carefully move the tree so that you can see all of the monkeys.) *"Yes you're right!"* (Clap for the monkeys who escaped.) Point to and count all of the monkeys. Cover them back up with the tree while saying, *"Let's keep them safe from the alligator."*

### FIVE LITTLE MONKEYS SWINGING FROM THE TREE

Five little monkeys  *(Hold up hand.)*
Swinging from the tree. *(Wave hand.)*
Teasing Mr. Alligator,
*"Can't catch me. Can't catch me!"*

Along comes Mr. Alligator
Quietly as can be.

SNAP! (Clap hands.)

Four little monkeys... *(Hold up 4 fingers.)*
Three little monkeys... *(Hold up 3 fingers.)*
Two little monkeys... *(Hold up 2 fingers.)*
One little monkey... *(Hold up 1 finger.)*

# MORE ANIMALS

## MAKE

Elephant
Bird
Snake
Lion
Horse
Duck
Monkey

## ANIMAL PARADE

Have all of the animals for the parade in an envelop next to your felt board. (Use as many animals as you think your children are able to handle at one time.)

Tell the children that all of the animals are getting together for an *"Animal Parade."* Put the elephant on the far left side of the board. Say *"The elephant is going to be the leader of the parade. How does he move?"* (Everyone get up or stay sitting and move in place like the elephant.)

*"Next come the birds."* (Put the bird on the felt board after the elephant.) *Let's fly like the birds."* (Fly around in place.)

*"After the birds is the snake.* (Put the snake after the birds) *He wiggles along the ground. Let's wiggle like the snake."* (Do it.)

*"The lion is a big animal.* (Put the lion on the board.) *He roars as he walks. Let's be lions, making loud roars as we walk in the 'Animal Parade'."* (Do it and stop.)

*"The horse marches in the parade.* (Put horse on the board after the lion.) *"Let's pretend we're horses marching in the 'Parade.' Our legs have to bend really high."* (March in place like a horse. Put the duck on the board next.)

*"The ducks make a lot of noise as they waddle in the 'Animal Parade.' What do the ducks say? Let's squat down and pretend we're noisy ducks as we waddle behind the horse."* (Waddle in place.)

# MORE ANIMALS

*"The monkeys are the last animals in the 'Parade.'* (Put the monkey after the duck.) *They walk and swing their arms. Do they make sounds? Like what?* (Children can *'talk'* like the monkeys.) *OK, let's be monkeys who are really happy to be last in the 'Parade'."*

After the *'monkeys'* have stopped walking, point to each animal and have the children call out what it is and wave good-bye to it. As you do, put the animals back into the envelop.

**EXTENSION:** Tell the children a simplified version of the book, CAPS FOR SALE, by Esphyr Slobidkina.

# MORE ANIMALS

## MAKE

Children's favorite
animals

## ANIMAL NOISES

Have all of the animals behind the felt board. It is morning and they are waking up, ready to play and use their loud voices. *"Wake"* the first animal up and slowly *"walk"* him out and put him on the felt board. As you do say in a *"lion-type"* voice, *"Here comes the lion."* Encourage the children to roar like the lion. (Place the animal on the far side of the board.) Continue with the rest of the animals.

After all of the animals have woken up, point to them randomly and let the children make loud animal noises. Take each one off the board as you do.

Play again making quiet sounds because the animals are getting ready for bed.

## MAKE

5 monkeys
Bed

## FIVE LITTLE MONKEYS JUMPING ON THE BED

Put the bed in the middle of the felt board. Have the monkeys near you. Place them on the bed one at a time counting aloud as you do.

After all five monkeys are on the bed, start saying FIVE LITTLE MONKEYS JUMPING ON THE BED. As each monkey falls off the bed, take one and tumble him/her to the floor and tuck him/her back under your leg.

FIVE LITTLE MONKEYS JUMPING ON THE BED
Five little monkeys jumping on the bed
One fell off and bumped his head.
Mama called the doctor and the doctor said,
*"No more monkeys jumping on the bed."*

Four little monkeys jumping on the bed...
Three little monkeys jumping on the bed...
Two little monkeys jumping on the bed...
One little monkey jumping on the bed...

# MORE ANIMALS

## MAKE

Fox
Rabbit
Large tree

## MAKE

Large goat
Medium goat
Small goat
Troll
Bridge
Meadow

## PROPS

THREE BILLY
GOAT GRUFFS
book or copy of
STORY CARD

## RUN, RUN RABBIT

Put the large tree on the felt board. Have the fox in your hand and the rabbit nearby. Start saying RUN, RUN RABBIT with the children. As you do put the 'sly silver fox' on the board. As you say, *"Who was looking for a rabbit"* put the rabbit near the fox.

Say the second and third verses very fast. As you are saying the words, *"run"* the rabbit all around the board so that the fox does not catch him. Let the rabbit finally stop and hide behind the tree — safe from the fox. Clap for the rabbit!!

<u>RUN, RUN RABBIT</u>

There once was fox.
A sly silver fox.
Who was looking for a rabbit. *(Hand above eyes.)*

Run, run rabbit. *(Slap thighs or floor.)*
Run, run rabbit.
Run, run rabbit fast as you can.

Don't let him catch me. *(Hug yourself.)*
Don't let him catch me.
Don't let him put me in the rabbit stew.

Repeat last 2 verses.

## THREE BILLY GOATS GRUFF, Story Card

Duplicate the STORY CARD, glue it to a piece of construction paper and laminate or cover it with a piece of clear adhesive paper.

Encourage the children to say the repetitive lines. Put the bridge on the feltboard and the meadow on the right side of the bridge.

# THREE BILLY GOAT GRUFF
## by Paul Galdone

The story begins, **"Once upon a time there were three Billy Goats."** (Put the goats on the left side of the bridge.)

The story continues:

• The goats were hungry and wanted to go over the river to the meadow to eat grass and daisies.

• They had to cross the bridge where the hungry Troll lived. (Put Troll under the bridge.)

• The smallest goat went first. *"TRIP, TRAP, TRIP, TRAP."* (*"Walk"* smallest goat onto bridge.) The Troll roared, *"Who's that tripping over my bridge?"* Goat said, *"Oh, it's only I, the tiniest Billy Goat Gruff. And I'm going to the meadow to make myself fat."* Troll said, *"No you're not, for I'm going to gobble you up."* Goat persuaded the Troll not to eat him - he was too small. The Troll should wait for the second Billy Goat Gruff. The smallest goat walked to the meadow. (*"Walk"* goat to meadow.)

• Second goat went next. *"TRIP, TRAP, TRIP, TRAP."* (*"Walk"* medium goat onto bridge.) Repeat story line.

• Third goat went next. *"TRIP, TRAP, TRIP, TRAP."* (*"Walk"* largest goat onto bridge.) Repeat story line, except at the end, the big Billy Goat Gruff butts the Troll off the bridge.

• The third goat walks to the meadow and joins his brothers to eat grass and daisies. (*"Walk"* third goat to meadow.)

Five Little
Monkeys

Swinging
From the Tree

**Five Little
Monkeys
Swinging
From the Tree**

**Five Little
Monkeys
Swinging
From the Tree**

# Animal Parade

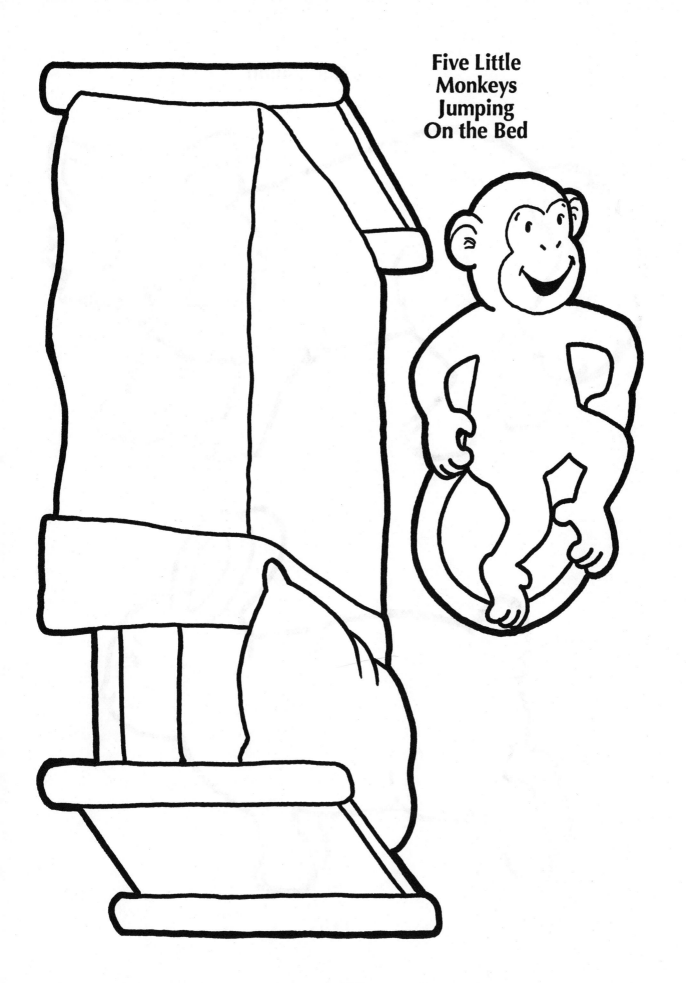

**Five Little
Monkeys
Jumping
On the Bed**

# Run, Run Rabbit

**Run, Run Rabbit**

# Three Billy
# Goats Gruff

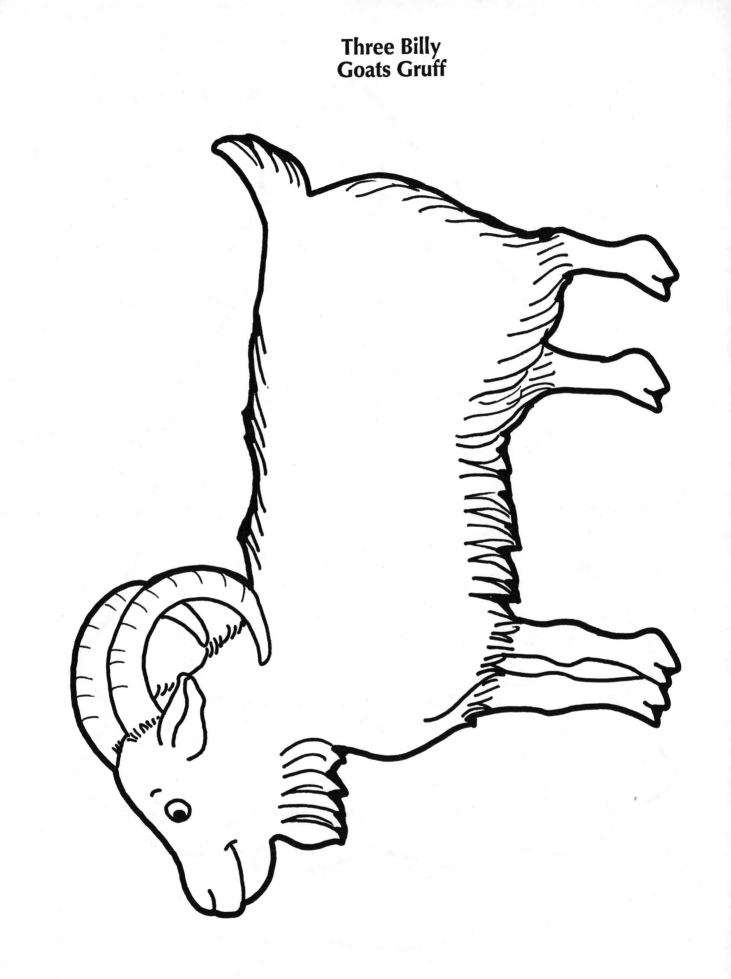

**Three Billy
Goats Gruff**

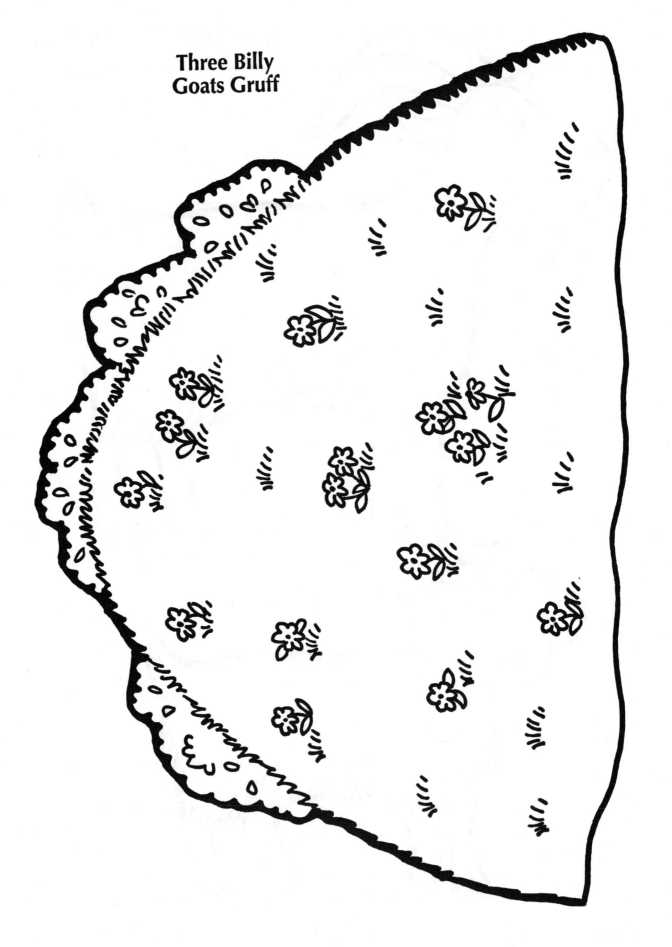

**Three Billy
Goats Gruff**

# TRANSPORTATION

## MAKE

Large cloud
Large pond
Railroad tracks
Road
Different colored
   vehicles:
   Airplane
   Rocket ship
   Engine
   Coal car
   Caboose
   Car
   Pick-up truck
   Tractor
   School bus
   Fire engine
   Motorcycle
   Rowboat
   Sailboat
   Motorboat

## MAKE

Car
Airplane
Bus
Fire engine
Rowboat
   from the activity,
   WHERE DO I
   BELONG?

## WHERE DO I BELONG?

Put two areas where the vehicles travel, such as the cloud and the road on your board. Put the cloud near the top left-side of your felt board and the road along the bottom on the right side. Have the vehicles which travel in the air and on the road tucked under your leg.

Put one vehicle in the middle of the board and say to the children, *"Does the blue airplane fly in the sky or drive on the road?"* (Fly it to the cloud.) As you're flying the felt airplane to the sky, encourage the children to be airplanes flying in the sky. Place another vehicle, such as the red truck, on the felt board and ask where it belongs. Continue until all of the vehicles are in the air or on the road.

Drive or fly the vehicles off the board encouraging the children to call out what they are, such as yellow bus, orange tractor, etc. Continue with two different areas or play again another day. Add the sounds that the vehicles make.

## FAST OR SLOW?

Have the vehicles behind the board. Put one vehicle, such as the fire engine, on the left side of your board.

Ask the children, *"Should I drive the fire engine fast or slow?"* They call out which one. Make the fire engine noise and drive it either fast or slow across the board. While you're driving your fire engine, let the children make fire engine noises and drive theirs too. Take the fire engine off the board. Put another vehicle on and play FAST OR SLOW again. (Remember to use the vehicles more than one time.)

# TRANSPORTATION

## MAKE

Bus
Rowboat
Fire engine
Train
    from the activity,
    WHERE DO I
    BELONG?

## PROPS

Chairs

## HURRY, HURRY

Set up chairs in a double aisle in front of the felt board. Stand by the felt board next to the chairs and put one of the vehicles, such as the fire engine, on the felt board. Call out, *"Hurry, hurry. Get aboard the fire engine"*. When everyone is aboard, sing LET'S BE FIREFIGHTERS as you drive down the street to the fire. After the song unload the fire engine and say *"Thanks for putting out that fire."* Put a different vehicle on the felt board and play and sing again.

### LET'S BE FIREFIGHTERS

(tune: 1 Little, 2 Little, 3 Little Children)

Hurry, hurry drive the fire truck. *(Drive.)*
Hurry, hurry drive the fire truck.
Hurry, hurry drive the fire truck.
On a Sunday morning.

Hurry, hurry turn the corner... *(Tip to one side.)*

Hurry, hurry find the fire... *(Look around.)*

Hurry, hurry climb the ladder... *(Hand over hand.)*

Hurry, hurry spray the water... *(Hold fire hose.)*

Hurry, hurry back to the station... *(Drive.)*

## ROW, ROW, ROW YOUR BOAT

Row, row, row your boat
Gently down the stream
Merrily, merrily, merrily, merrily
Life is but a dream.

## THE TRAIN

Choo, choo, choo *(Rotate arms forward.)*
The train comes down the track.
Choo, choo, choo *(Rotate arms backwards.)*
And runs right back.

## MAKE
Grandma
Two girls
Two winter coats
Bus
Taxi

## PROPS
WHEELS ON THE
BUS book or copy
of the STORY
CARD

# WHEELS ON THE BUS, Story Card

Duplicate the STORY CARD, glue it to a piece of construction paper, and laminate or cover it with clear adhesive paper. Tell the story and sing the song.

# WHEELS ON THE BUS
## by Maryann Kovalski

The story begins "One day, Grandma took Jenny and Joanna shopping for new winter coats."

The story continues

**They tried on long coats - short coats**
**blue coats - red coats**
**even raincoats**

Joanne chooses a coat with wooden barrel buttons. Jenny liked it too because of the hood. When it was time to go home they waited for the bus.

As they waited Grandma taught them the song, THE WHEELS ON THE BUS

The wheels on the bus go round and round...

The wipers on the bus go swish, swish, swish...

The people on the bus hop up and off...

The horn on the bus goes toot, toot, toot...

The money on the bus goes clink, clink, clink...

The people on the bus hop up and down...

The babies on the bus go waa, waa, waa...

The parents on the bus go shh, shh, shh...

The wheels on the bus go round and round...

Jenny, Joanna, and Grandma had so much fun they missed the bus and had to take a taxi home.

# Where Do I
# Belong

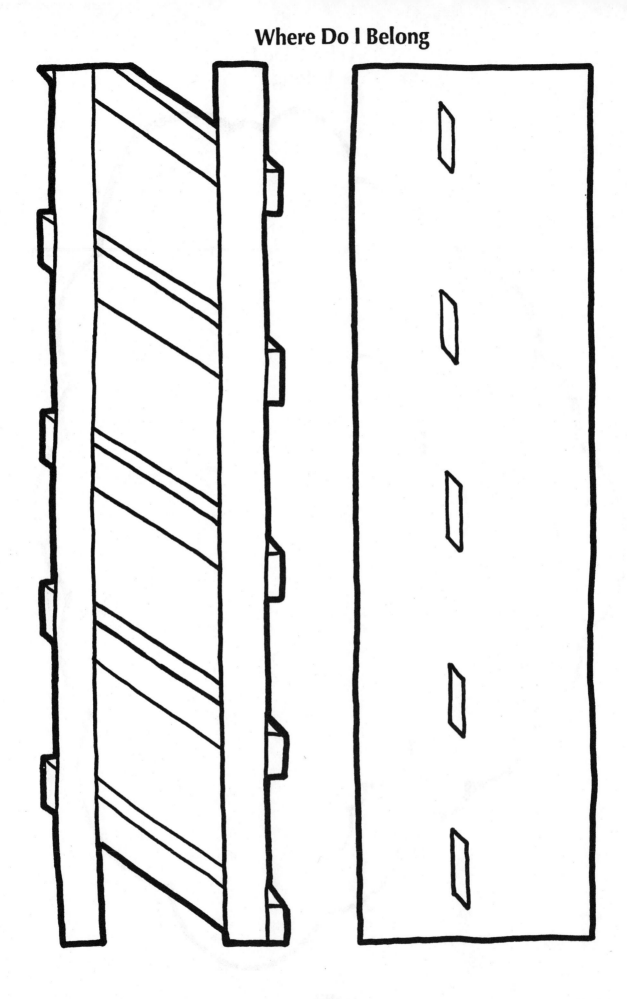

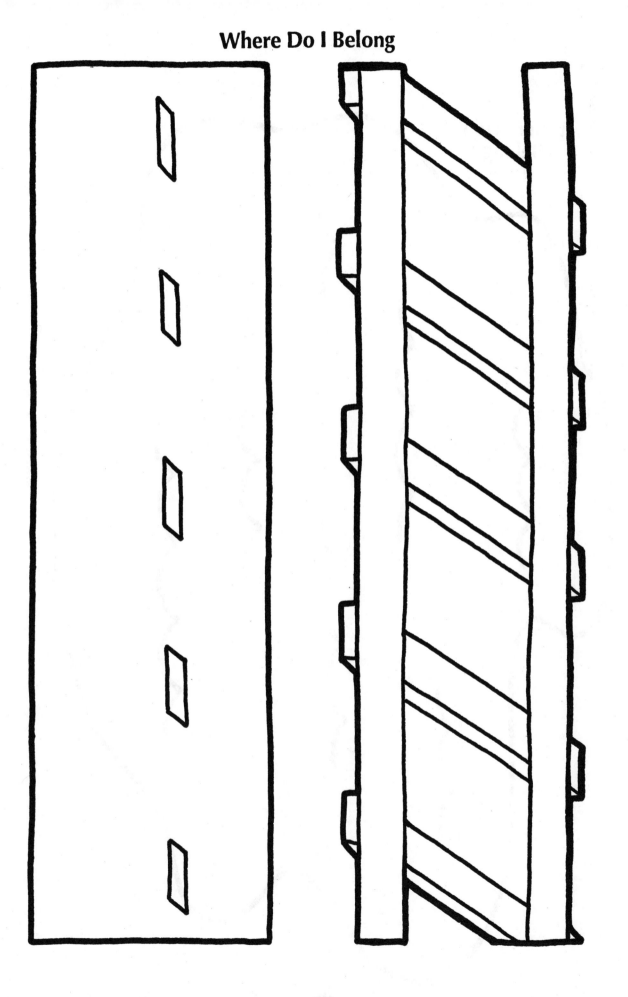

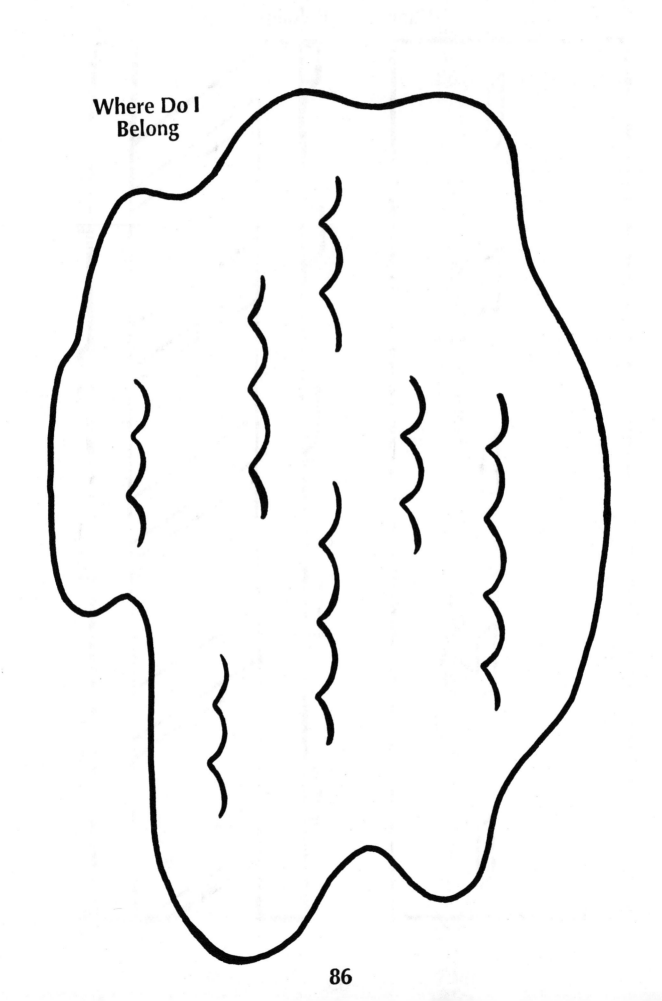

Where Do I
Belong

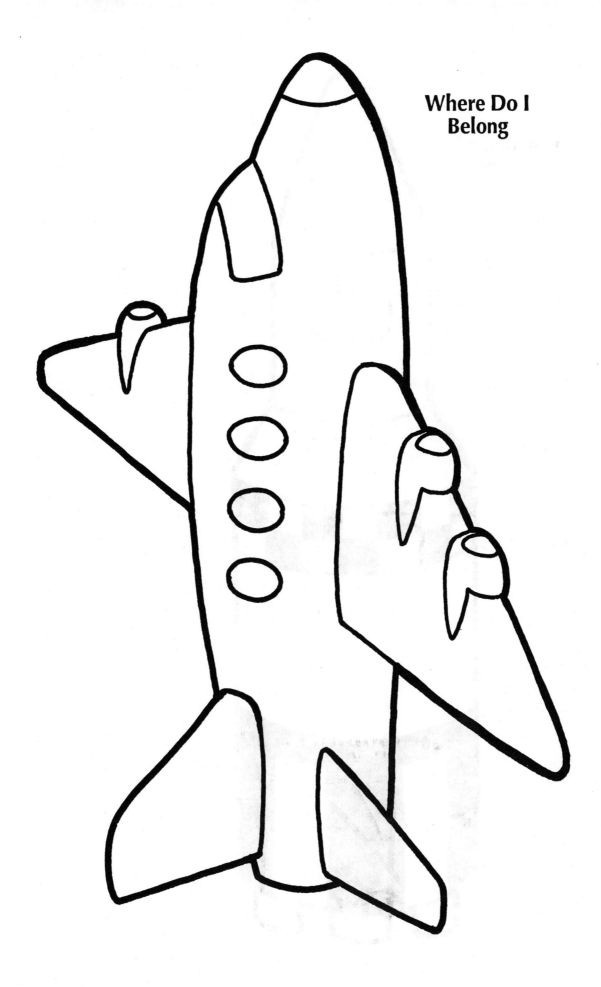

**Where Do I Belong**

**Where Do I Belong**

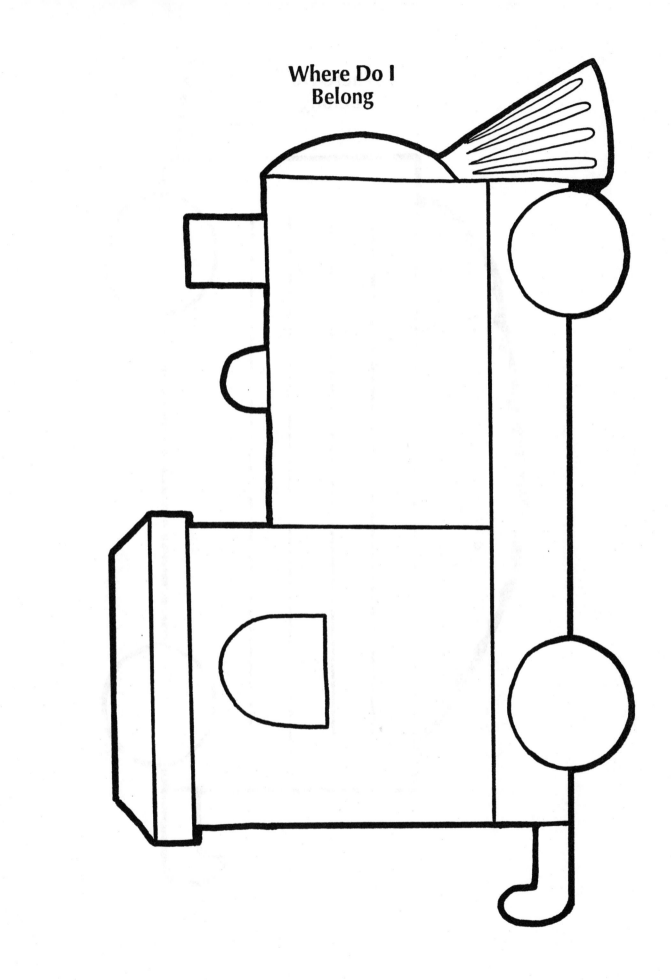

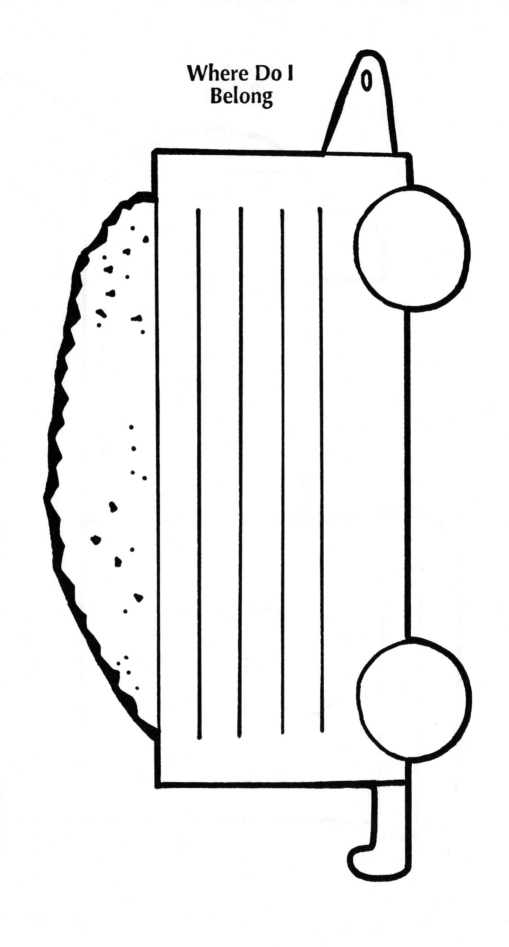

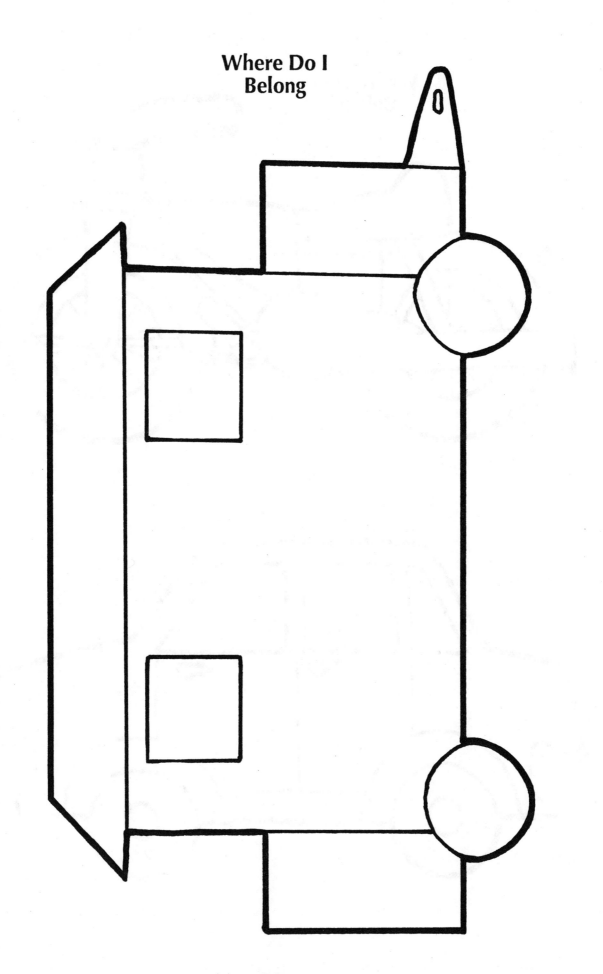

# Where Do I
# Belong

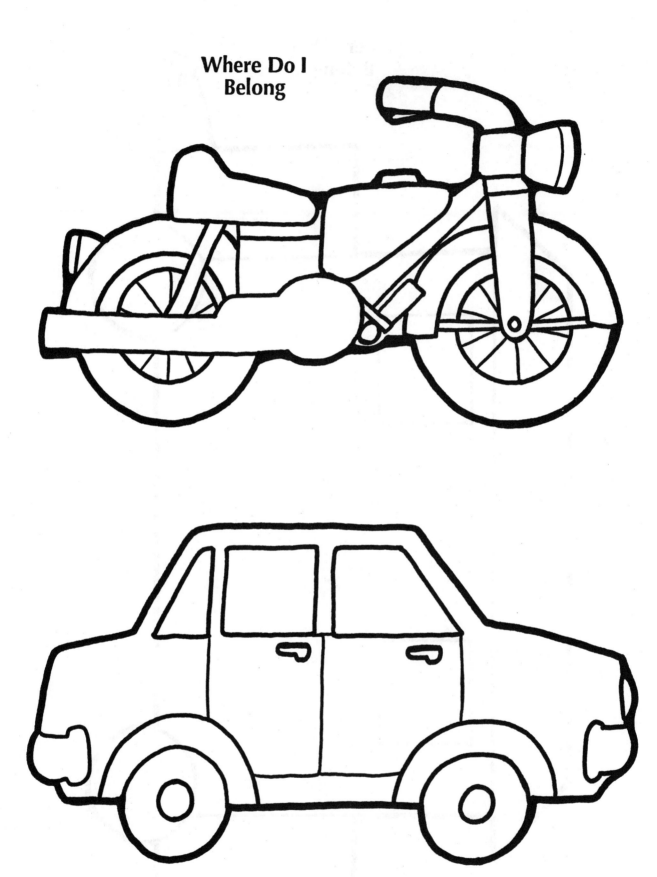

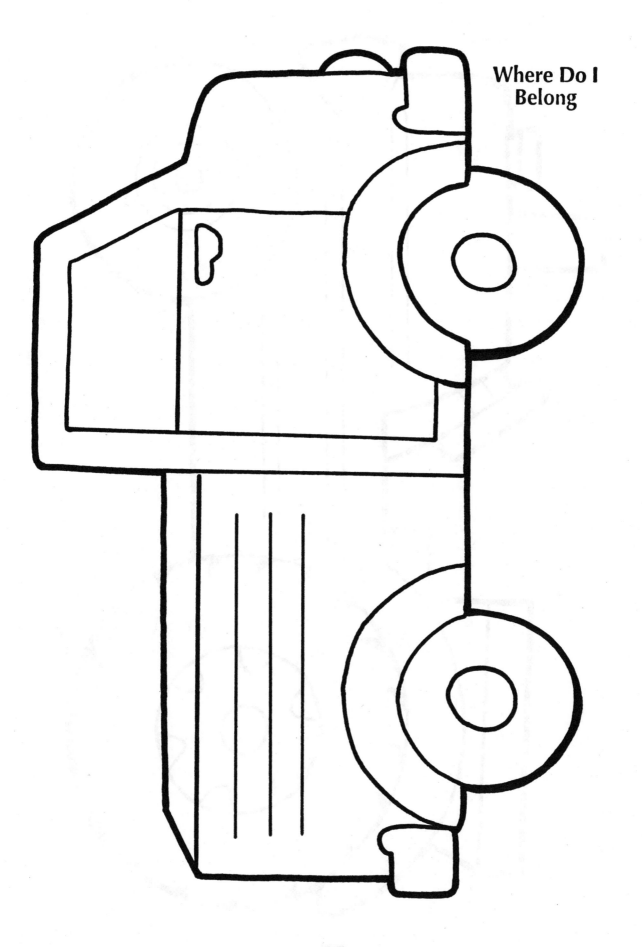

**Where Do I Belong**

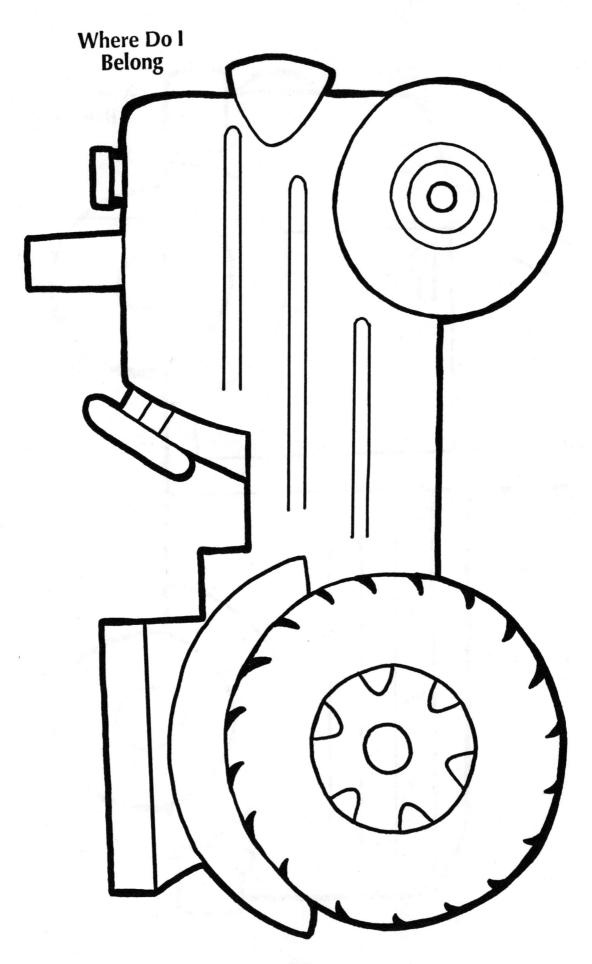

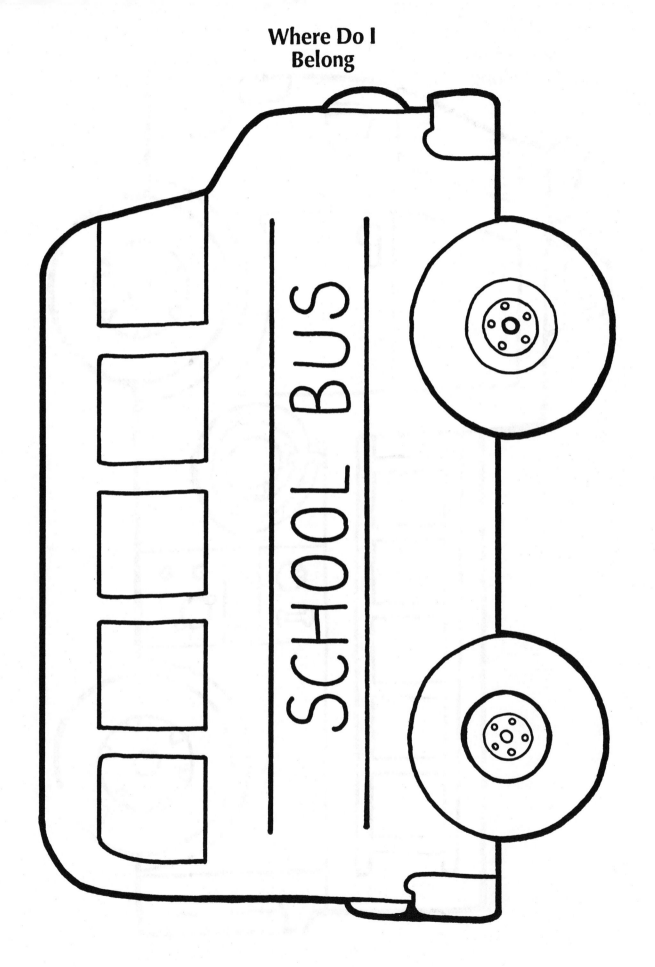

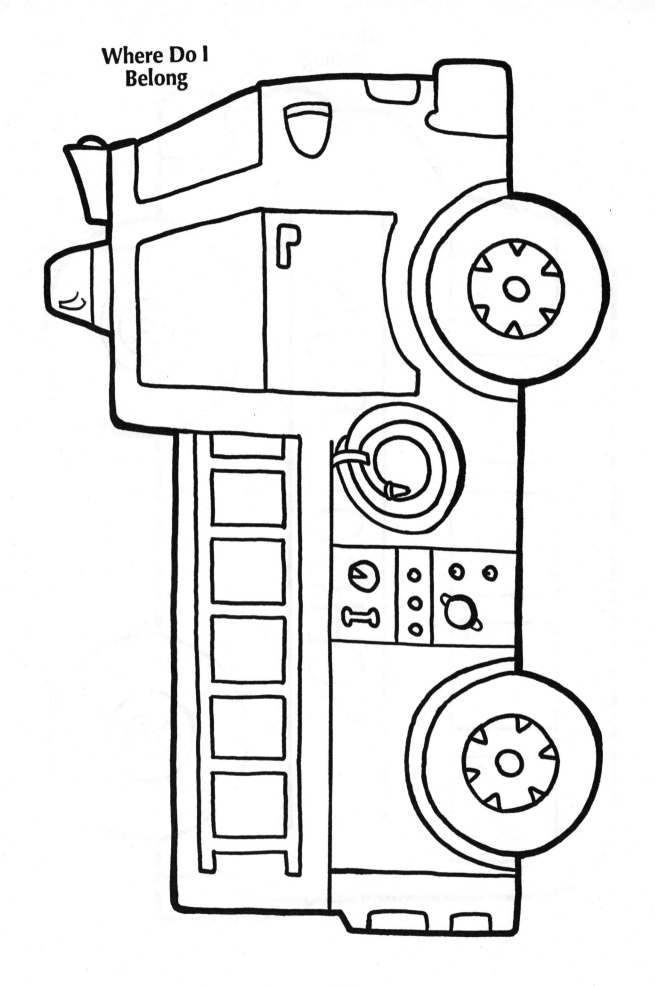

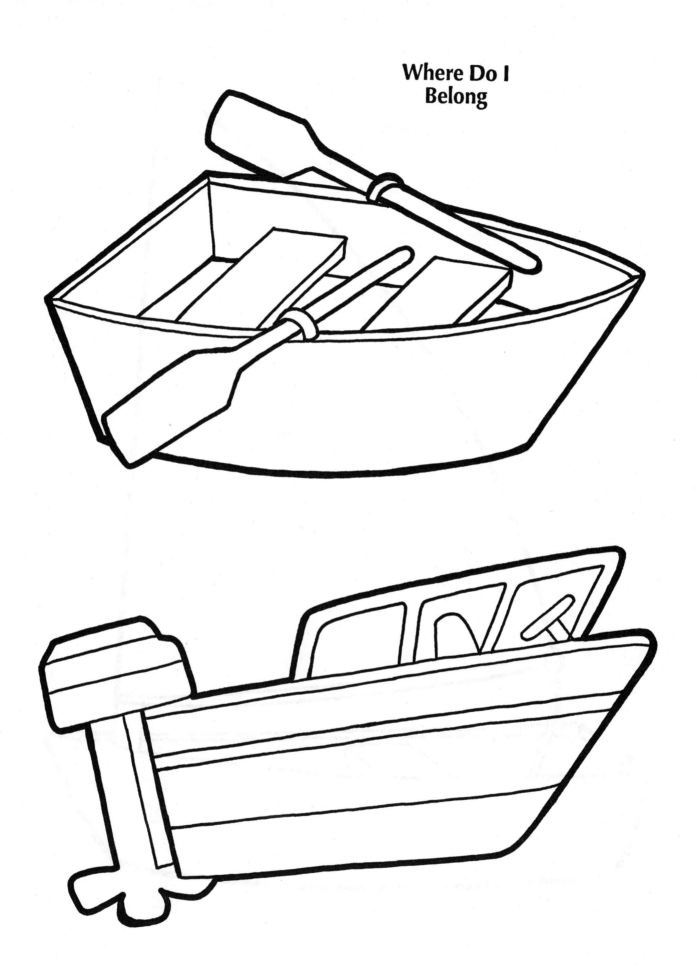

# Where Do I
# Belong

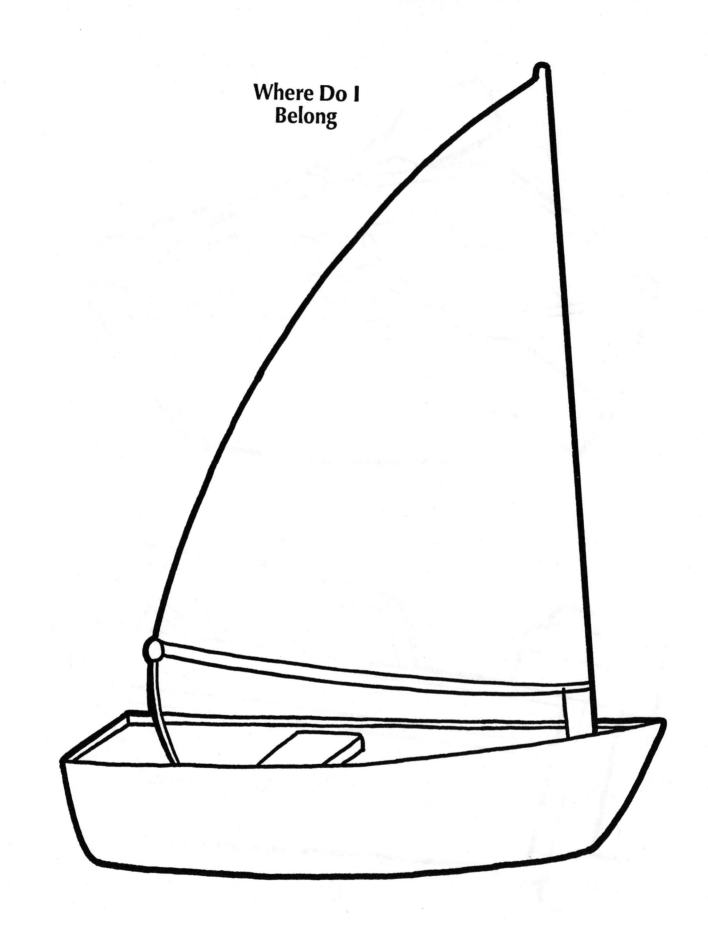

# Wheels On the
# Bus

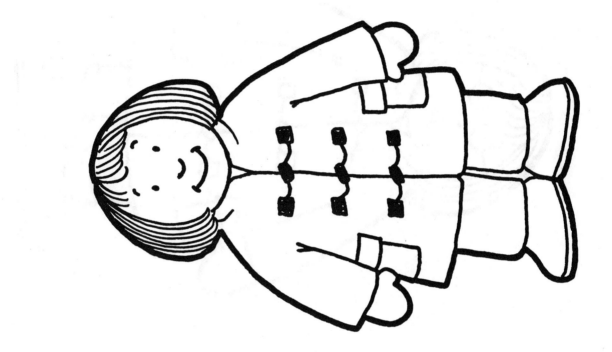

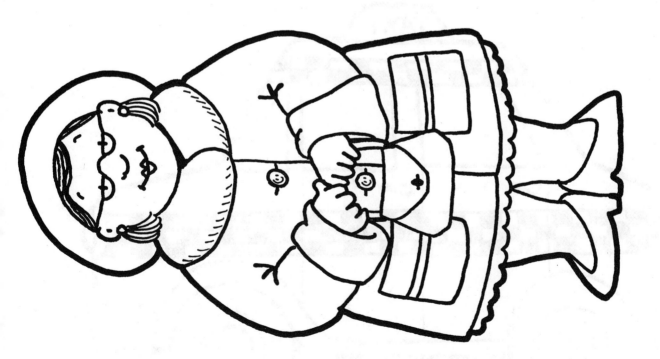

99

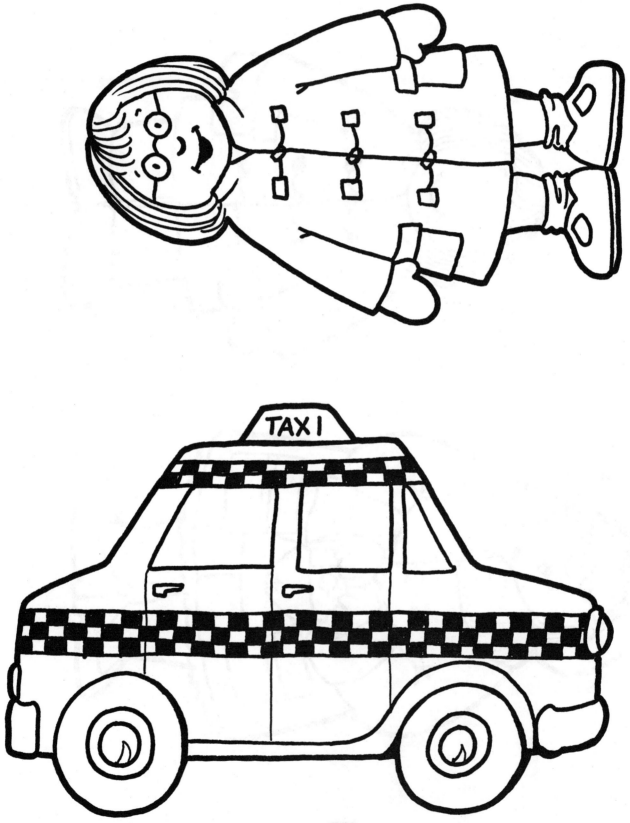

# Wheels On the Bus

THE TOWN BUS COMPANY

# FOOD

## MAKE

Huge tree
2 smiling apples

## PROPS

Several real apples
Knife (safety)
Cutting board

## APPLE TREE

Put the tree on the felt board and hold the apples. Say APPLE TREE with the children. As you're saying it actively use your felt board.

- Point to *"high"* in the apple tree.

- Place the *"two smiling apples"* high in the tree.

- *"Shake"* the felt board until the apples (and probably the tree) fall off.

Place the tree back on the felt board. Bring out the real apples, a cutting board, and a knife. Talk about the real apple, while you're cutting it into bite-size slices. Pass a slice to each child. Enjoy the apples and then say APPLE TREE again.

VARIATION: Instead of eating the apple slices, make applesauce with the children and have it for snack with a cracker.

### APPLE TREE

Way up high in the apple tree
Two little apples smiled at me.

I shook that tree as hard as I could.
Down came the apples.

Ummmmmm! Ummmmmm! GOOD!

# FOOD

## MAKE

2 slices of bread
Several peanuts
Bunch of grapes

## PROPS

Dull knife
Jar of jelly
Jar of peanut
Butter
Bread
Cutting board

## PEANUT BUTTER AND JELLY SANDWICH

Sing PEANUT BUTTER AND JELLY with the children. As you sing about *"smushing"* the peanuts and *"smashing"* the grapes, put the large felt peanuts and bunch of grapes on the felt board. At the end when you are making your sandwich, put one slice of bread on the board, add the grapes and peanuts, and cover the sandwich with the second piece of bread. Ask the children if that's what their peanut butter and jelly sandwiches look like? Is it a silly sandwich?

EXTENSIONS:

• Have a bunch of purple or red grapes which you've washed. Let the children taste them. Have a bag of peanuts in the shells. Sometime during the day shell the nuts with the children and let them taste a peanut or two. Remember to chew them well. (Instead of eating them right away use the peanuts to make peanut butter with the children.)

• Make several peanut butter and jelly sandwiches ahead of time. Cut them into bite- size pieces. After singing let each child have her own *"mini-sandwich."*

• Make a sandwich as you sing. As you sing each verse bring out the ingredients. At the end spread the peanut butter and jelly on the bread. Cover it with the second piece of bread. Cut the sandwich into tiny pieces so that each child can have a *"taste."*

**104**

# FOOD

## PEANUT BUTTER AND JELLY

Peanut, peanut butter — and jelly
　*(Shout peanut; whisper jelly.)*
Peanut, peanut butter — and jelly
Peanut, peanut butter — and jelly.

First you take a peanut and you smush it,
Smush it. *(Rub hands together.)*
First you take a peanut and you smush it,
Smush it.

Peanut, peanut butter — and jelly......*(Hum)*

Next you take the grapes and you smash them,
Smash them. *(Rub hands together.)*
Next you take the grapes and you smash them,
Smash them.

Peanut, peanut butter — and jelly...... *(Hum.)*

Then you take a knife and you spread them,
Spread them.
　*(Spread one palm with opposite fingers.)*
Then you take a knife and you spread them,
Spread them.

Peanut, peanut butter — and jelly......*(Hum.)*

Then you take the sandwich and you bite it,
Bite it. *(Chew.)*
Then you take the sandwich and you bite it,
Bite it.

Peanut, peanut butter — and jelly......*(Hum.)*

# FOOD

## MAKE

Foods that you children will recognize from each food category

## NAME THAT FOOD

Put 4 or 5 felt pieces of recognizable food from each food group behind the board. Bring out the foods from one group. Put all of the pieces on the board. Tell the children that all of these are *"vegetables."* Name a child and everyone chant, *"Child's name, what vegetable do you see?"* Child names any vegetable he wants. Continue chanting and letting the children name the vegetables.

Continue the game by removing the vegetable group and putting up another food group.

# FOOD

## MAKE

Leaf
Egg
Caterpillar
Sun
Apple
Pear
Plum
Strawberry
Orange
Chocolate cake
Ice cream cone
Pickle
Cheese
Salami
Lollipop
Cherry pie
Sausage
Cupcake
Watermelon
Cocoon
Butterfly

## PROPS

Real or plastic fruit
    in a basket
Smelling jars for
    each fruit
Long knee sock
VERY HUNGRY
    CATERPILLAR
    book or copy of
    the STORY CARD

## VERY HUNGRY CATERPILLAR, Story Card

Duplicate the STORY CARD, glue it to a piece of construction paper and laminate or cover it with clear adhesive paper.

Put the large leaf on the felt board with the caterpillar on the edge of it. Have all of the foods in order behind the board. Tell the children the story in a variety of ways.

• FELT STORY: The first several times that you tell the story to your children, put the felt pieces on the board as you tell it. Begin with the big leaf. Quickly name and place each food that the caterpillar eats on the leaf. After he's eaten all of the food, point to each one in the order in which he ate it and quickly rename the foods with the children. As you do take each food off the leaf.

Continue telling the story as you *secretively* lay the butterfly on the leaf and the cocoon over the top of the leaf hiding the butterfly. The caterpillar spins his cocoon. Slowly and carefully take the cocoon off the board. Surprise! A beautiful butterfly! Everyone clap for the new butterfly and celebrate by being butterflies flying around the room.

• TASTING PARTY: Before telling the story cut up small pieces of each fruit. Put each of them in a separate bowl. (Keep them refrigerated if necessary.)

Put the felt leaf and caterpillar on the felt board. Begin telling the story. As you name each fruit let the children taste it. Continue until the caterpillar and your children have eaten enough to curl up into a cocoon. Add the butterfly, cover the leaf, and finish the story.

VARIATIONS:

Instead of having a tasting party while telling the story, have a basket of real fruit. Hold up each fruit as you tell the story. After the story, wash your hands, cut up the fruit with the children, and then have your tasting party.

Another time tell the story using the plastic food from the housekeeping area instead of real food.

# FOOD

• **TELL AND SMELL:** Before telling the story make smelling jars. (Get a film canister or other small container with a lid for each food. Poke a hole in each lid. Put a piece of cotton in each one. Cut a piece of food. Put one in each container. Cover the canisters. Put them on a tray in the order in which you tell the story.)

Put the felt leaf and caterpillar on the board. Begin telling the story. When it's time to name the first food, let the children smell the food in the first canister. *"What food do you smell?"* Continue telling the story and smelling and naming each food.

After smelling and naming the last food, cover the butterfly and leaf with the cocoon and finish the story.

• **PUPPET STORY:** Put the long puppet (knee sock) on your arm. *"Secretively"* put the butterfly piece in your hand and close it up, so that your children can't see it. Tell the story, putting the pieces on the stocking along the length of your arm. At the end open your hand as the butterfly emerges.

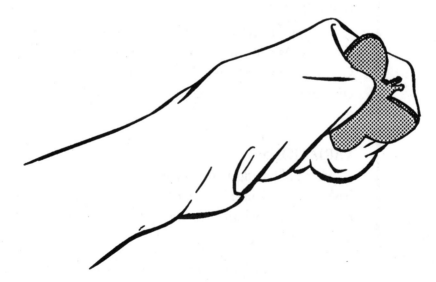

# THE VERY HUNGRY CATERPILLAR
## by Eric Carle

The story begins: *"In the light of the moon, a little egg lay on a leaf."*

The story continues:

• On Sunday morning the sun came up and - pop! - a tiny, hungry caterpillar came out of the egg.

• He ate

| | |
|---|---|
| On Monday - | 1 apple |
| On Tuesday - | 2 pears |
| On Wednesday | 3 plums |
| On Thursday | 4 strawberries |
| On Friday - | 5 oranges |
| On Saturday - | 1 piece of chocolate cake |
| | 1 ice cream cone |
| | 1 pickle |
| | 1 slice Swiss cheese |
| | 1 slice salami |
| | 1 lollipop |
| | 1 piece of cherry pie |
| | 1 sausage |
| | 1 cupcake |
| | 1 slice of watermelon |

He felt sick
On Sunday he ate the green leaf and felt better.

• He was a big caterpillar.

• He built a cocoon.

• After two weeks he nibbled a hole in his cocoon and pushed out.

• He emerged as a beautiful butterfly.

# Apple Tree

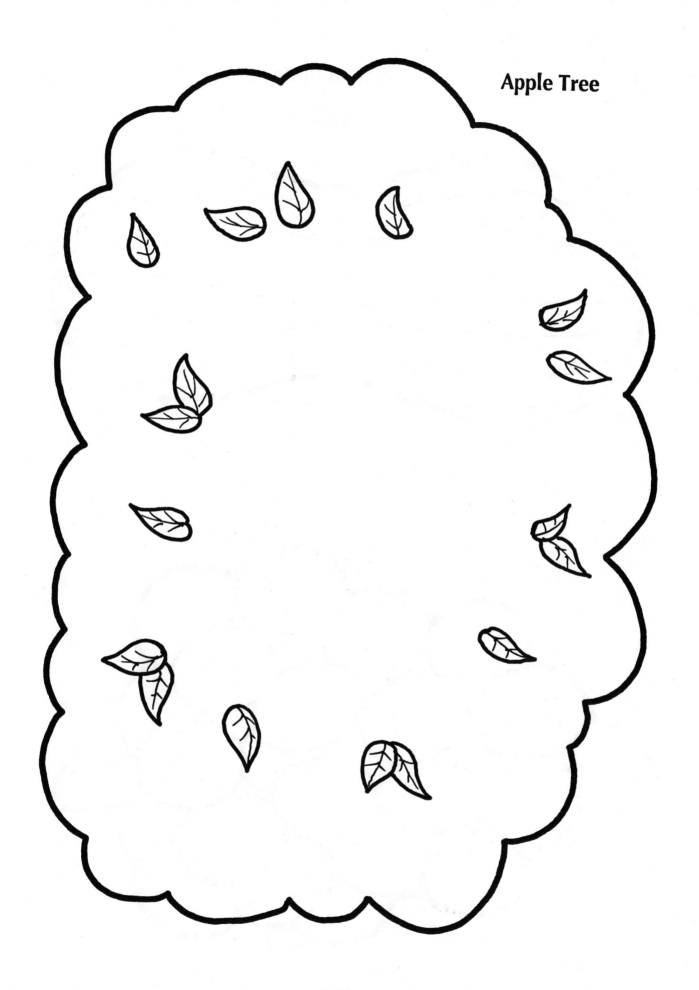

**Apple Tree**

# Peanut Butter
## and Jelly
## Sandwich

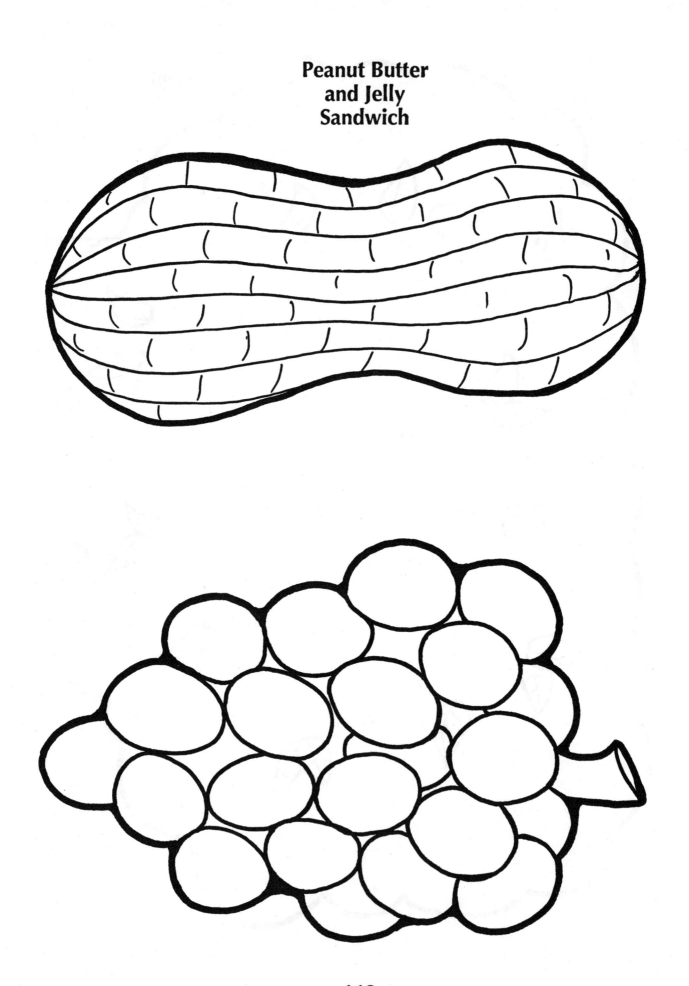

# Peanut Butter
# and Jelly
# Sandwich

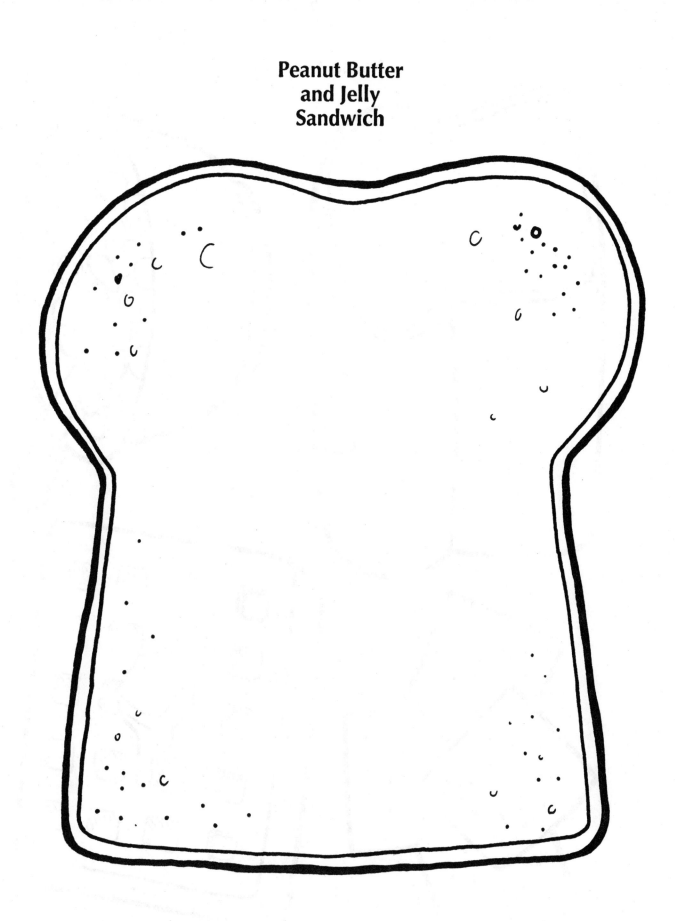

**Name That Food**

# Name That Food

KETCHUP

CORN
OIL

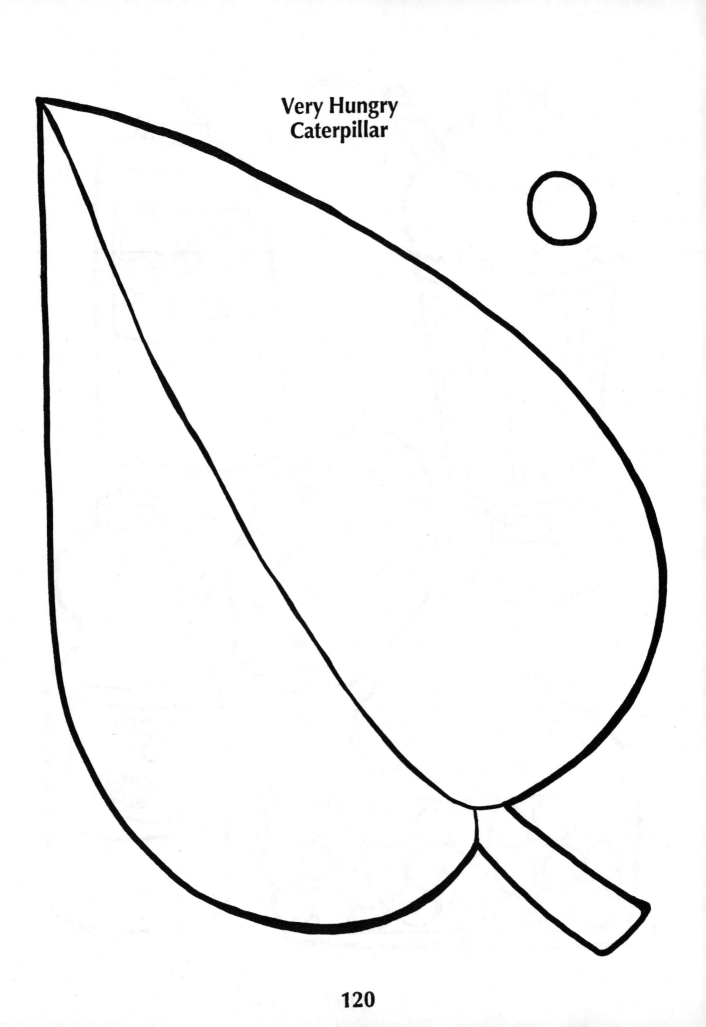

**Very Hungry
Caterpillar**

**Very Hungry Caterpillar**

# Very Hungry Caterpillar

**Very Hungry
Caterpillar**

# MY BODY

## MAKE

Boy
Girl
2 shirts
Shorts
2 pairs of shoes
2 pairs of socks
Blue jeans

Additional clothes:
  Sweatpants
  Sweatshirt
  Sweater
  Skirt

## TERRI AND TOBY GET DRESSED

Put Terri and Toby on the felt board. Have their felt clothes behind the board. Tell your children that Terri and Toby just woke up and they are going to get dressed.

Toby is going to get dressed first. (Take Terri off the board.) Put all of Toby's clothes to one side of the board, naming each one as you do. Dress Toby in the order in which your children get dressed. For example, say to the children, *"First Toby is going to put on his 'red' shirt.* (Do it.) *How many of your put your shirts on first?* (Talk.) *Next he's going to put on his 'black' shorts.* (Do it.) *Do any of you wear shorts?"* (Talk.) Continue dressing Toby until he's ready to play.

Put Terri on the felt board along with her clothes. Point to each article of her clothing and name it while your children point to theirs. Put Terri's shirt on first and say to your children, *"Terri's wearing her blue shirt today. Let's see what color shirts each of you are wearing today."* (Quickly point to each child and say the child's name and the color shirt he is wearing.) Next put on her jeans. Ask your children, *"Who's wearing jeans today?"* (Name them.) *Who's not wearing jeans?"* (Name those children.) Continue dressing Terri until she's ready to play with Toby.

EXTENSION: Dress Terri and Toby on other days using a variety of other clothes.

# MY BODY

## MAKE

Boy
Girl

Summer
    T-shirt
    Boy's swimsuit
    Girl's swimsuit

Winter
    Snowmobile suit
    2-piece snow suit
    Snow boots
    Mittens
    Stocking cap

Fall
    Hooded sweat
Jacket
    Sweater
    Jacket

Spring
    Raincoat
    Rain hat
    Umbrella

Use clothes from
    the activity
    TERRI AND
    TOBY GET
    DRESSED.

## ALI & AARON DRESS FOR THE SEASON

Put the boy and girl on the felt board. Have the felt clothes for the different seasons behind the board. Each time you do this activity tell your children a different story about the weather and what activity the children were going to do. After the short story bring out the appropriate set of clothes and dress the felt children for the weather and the activity. Here are some stories to start with.

• **PLAYING IN THE SNOW:** It was snowing and Ali and Aaron wanted to go outside. They ran to their mom and said, *"We want to go outside."* She said, *"Yes, let's all go out and build a snow person."* Ali and Aaron started to open the door, but their mom called, *"We've got to put on our snow clothes first."* (Dress the children for snow.)

• **LET'S GO SWIMMING:** It was very hot and Ali and Aaron wanted to go swimming in their pool. Their dad said, *"Oh, no. I forgot to put water in it. I'm sorry. How about all of us go outside and play in the water from the hose."* Ali and Aaron were so excited they jumped up and down and then raced off to put on their bathing suits. (Dress the children for playing with water.)

• **RAKING THE LEAVES:** Ali and Aaron were looking out one of their big windows at the leaves blowing in the wind. Their mom came in the room and said, *"Let's go outside and rake the leaves into a big pile. When it's big enough we'll run and jump into it!"* (Dress the children for raking leaves.)

• Tell other simple stories about:
    - Going To the Store
    - Visiting the Zoo
    - Going To the Park
    - Having a Picnic
    - Splashing In Puddles

# MY BODY

## MAKE

Girl
Use the clothes
from the activity
TERRI AND TOBY
GET DRESSED

## MOVE YOUR BODY

Put Maria on the felt board along with her clothes. Name each piece of clothing as you slowly dress her. Let your children pretend to get dressed by putting each piece of clothing on themselves, as you dress Maria.

After Maria is dressed, say to your children, *"Maria is ready to play. Let's play with her."*

• *"First she's going to flap her arms* (point to Maria's arms) *and pretend she's a bird flying around the room."* (Do this with the children and come back to the felt board.)

• *"Now Maria is going to use her legs* (point to Maria's legs) *to march like a soldier in a parade. Let's march around the table."* (Do it and come back to the felt board.)

• *"Maria saw some clowns on television. They were sitting on the floor bending their waists in all directions."* (Point to Maria's waist. Have the children sit down and bend side to side and front to back.)

• *"While Maria and her Dad were playing in the park, some other children were ice skating. Let's use our legs* (point to legs) *and skate over to the door and back again."* (Do it and come back to the felt board.)

• Continue with other movements. Do them in place or around the room.

# MY BODY

## MAKE

Child
Pair of shoes
Socks
Shirt
Pants

## PROPS

5-6 shirts
5-6 loose pants
5-6 large socks
5-6 large shoes

## THIS IS THE WAY WE PUT ON OUR CLOTHES

Put a felt child on the board and have the clothes tucked under your leg. Sing THIS IS THE WAY WE PUT ON OUR CLOTHES with the children. As you sing each verse, dress the felt child and have your children pretend to put the clothes on their bodies.

Bring out a PROP BOX filled with real clothes to match the ones in the song. Sing again. Just before you start each verse pass out the particular piece of clothing to the children. As you sing have the children put on the clothes. Repeat with each verse. (Take the children's picture at the end.)

### THIS IS THE WAY WE PUT ON OUR CLOTHES
*(tune: Here We Go Round the Mulberry Bush)*

This is the way we put on our shirts,
Put on our shorts, put on our shirts.
This is the way we put on our shirts,
So early in the morning.

This is the way we put on our pants...

This is the way we put on our socks...

This is the way we put on our shoes...

VARIATION: Each time you do this activity put out a different combination of clothes. Change the words of the song to match the clothes you're using.

**132**

# MY BODY

## MAKE

Boy
Use the clothes
from the
activities TERRI
AND TOBY GET
DRESSED and
ALI AND
AARON DRESS
FOR THE
SEASON.

## MAKE

Use children and
clothes from the
activities TERRI
AND TOBY GET
DRESSED and
ALI AND
AARON DRESS
FOR THE
SEASON

## NAME THE BODY PARTS

Put the felt child on the board. Have his clothes tucked under your leg.

Say to your children, "(Name), *is going to put on his shirt. What body parts will he cover up?"* After the children name them, put the felt child's shirt on. Continue naming body parts as he puts on his other clothes.

## HANDS IN YOUR POCKETS

Put a child on the felt board. Have the clothes tucked under your leg.

Dress the child. As you do, talk about the features of her clothes, such as pockets in her pants and buttons on her shirt. Have your children find the *"features"* on their clothes. *"What do they have in their pockets?"*

EXTENSION: Play a simple game called, HANDS IN YOUR POCKETS. Say to the children, *"Put your hands in your pockets. - Take your hands out of your pockets. - put your hands in your pockets."* Continue mixing up *"in"* and *"out"* of the pockets. (If some children do not have pockets encourage them to pretend they do.)

# MY BODY

## MAKE

Teddy bear
Shirt
Pants
Cap
Shoes

## HOW DO I PUT IT ON, Story Card

Duplicate the STORY CARD, glue it to a piece of construction paper, and laminate or cover it with clear adhesive paper.

Put the Teddy Bear on the felt board. Have Teddy Bear's felt clothes tucked under your leg. As you tell the story, dress the Bear, first the wrong way and then the right way. Encourage the children to chime in with the repetitive line. *"NO!"*

# HOW DO I PUT IT ON
## Shigeo Watanabe

The story begins:
*"I can get dressed all by myself. This is my shirt."*

- **Shirt**

  Bear puts shirt on legs. *("NO!")*
  Bear puts shirt on stomach.

- **Pants**

  Bear puts pants on stomach  *("NO!")*
  Bear puts pants on legs.

- **Cap**

  Bear puts cap on foot. *("NO!")*
  Bear puts cap on head.

- **Shoes**

  Bear puts shoes on ears. *("NO!")*
  Bear puts shoes on feet.

- **Bears**

- Takes all of his clothes off and dresses again.

- *("I'm ready. Off I go!")*

135

**Terri and Toby
Get Dressed**

# Terri and Toby
# Get Dressed

# Terri and Toby
# Get Dressed

**Ali and Aaron Dress For the Season**

**Ali and Aaron Dress For the Season**

# Ali and Aaron
## Dress For the
## Season

**Ali and Aaron
Dress For the
Season**

**Ali and Aaron
Dress For the
Season**

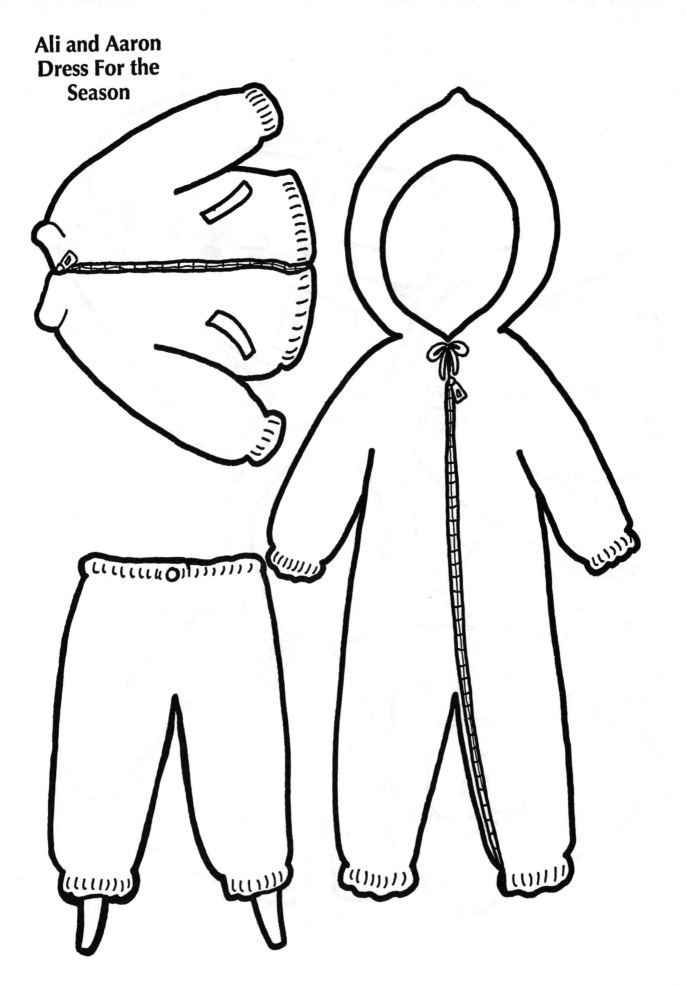

Move Your
Body

147

# HAPPY BIRTHDAY

## MAKE

4 or more children
Same number of
    different-colored
    party hats

## BIRTHDAY HATS

Tuck all of the felt children under your leg and have the colored party hats behind the felt board.

Put one felt child on the board. Say to your children, *"Today we're going to have a birthday party and invite lots of our friends. Oh good, here comes our first friend."* (Put one felt child on the board. Have your children pretend to *"knock"* on the door by shaking their fists and clucking their tongues.) You say, *"(Name), welcome to the birthday party! Here, put on a red birthday hat."* As you are talking, put the red felt hat on the child's head. Continue telling the story until all of the felt children have arrived and are wearing the different-colored birthday hats.

Have the party:
- Sing HAPPY BIRTHDAY several times.
- Hold up several fingers and pretend that they are the birthday candles. Blow them out.
- Play RING AROUND THE ROSIE.

Soon it's time for the children to go home. Take off each child's hat. As you do have everyone call out the color. Now take the felt children off the board, while your children wave good-bye and you say good-bye — *"Thanks for coming. — Bye now — Buenos dias"* etc.

# HAPPY BIRTHDAY

## MAKE

4 children from the
activity
BIRTHDAY
HATS

## PROPS

4 different size and
shaped boxes
A toy which fits in
each box

## BIRTHDAY PRESENTS

Place the toys in the boxes. Put the birthday children and the birthday presents behind the felt board. Say to your children, *"These children are going to a birthday party."* (Put all four children on the felt board.) Each of them is bringing a present.

*"(Name) is bringing a birthday present in a large, square box."* (Bring this box out to show the children.) Continue in this manner, naming the size and shape of each box, until you've brought out all four boxes.

After all the felt children have gifts, say, *"Time to open the presents."* Point to the first gift. Talk about what it could be. Then open it up and show the children. Point to another gift, *'open'* it up, and talk about what it could be. Open it. Continue with the remaining gifts.

Everyone sing HAPPY BIRTHDAY and pretend to blow out the candles.

# HAPPY BIRTHDAY

## MAKE

Birthday cake
1 candle
Young child

## FIRST BIRTHDAY

Put the young child on the felt board and the cake and candle behind it. Tell the children about this child's first birthday party.

*"Today my friend Charlie is celebrating her first birthday. See, she even has a number 1 on her shirt. I have brought her a birthday cake.* (Put it on the board.) *What kind do you think I made for her?* (Talk with the children.) *Because she's one, I'm going to put one candle on it.* (Do it.) *Let's clap as we sing HAPPY BIRTHDAY."* (Clap and sing.)

After you've sung it once in a normal voice, say, *"Let's clap and sing again, only this time let's use our whisper voices. Shhh!"* (Clap and sing again.) Blow out the one candle (take off cake) and clap for the first birthday.

## MAKE

Birthday cake
Candles

## HAPPY BIRTHDAY

Put the birthday cake on the felt board, as you say to the children, *"It's time for birthday cake."* Put two candles on it while counting aloud, *"1, 2."* (The children who want will count with you.) Then everyone sing HAPPY BIRTHDAY and blow out the candles. Say to the children, *"Oops you missed one candle. Blow again."* (Do it.) *"Good, you got the other one."* Take the candles off the cake. Clap for the birthday!!

Play again and again putting different numbers of candles on the cake.

# HAPPY BIRTHDAY

## MAKE

Clown
Bucket
4 to 8 different
　　colored circles

## BUSTER'S BIRTHDAY BUCKETS

Put *"Buster"* on the left side of your felt board along with all of the colored balls around his feet. Place the bucket on the right side of the felt board.

Say to the children, *"Buster is playing a game at a birthday party. He is trying to toss the colored balls into the bucket. He needs our help. Buster wants us to call out a color. He'll toss the one we tell him."* Have the children name a color. You pick up that ball and slowly *"toss"* it towards the bucket and lay it on top. Continue until all of the colored balls are in the bucket. Clap for Buster!!

Point to each ball and have everyone call out what color it is. As you say the color, take it out of the bucket, and give it back to Buster.

# Birthday Hats

HAPPY BIRTHDAY!

# First Birthday

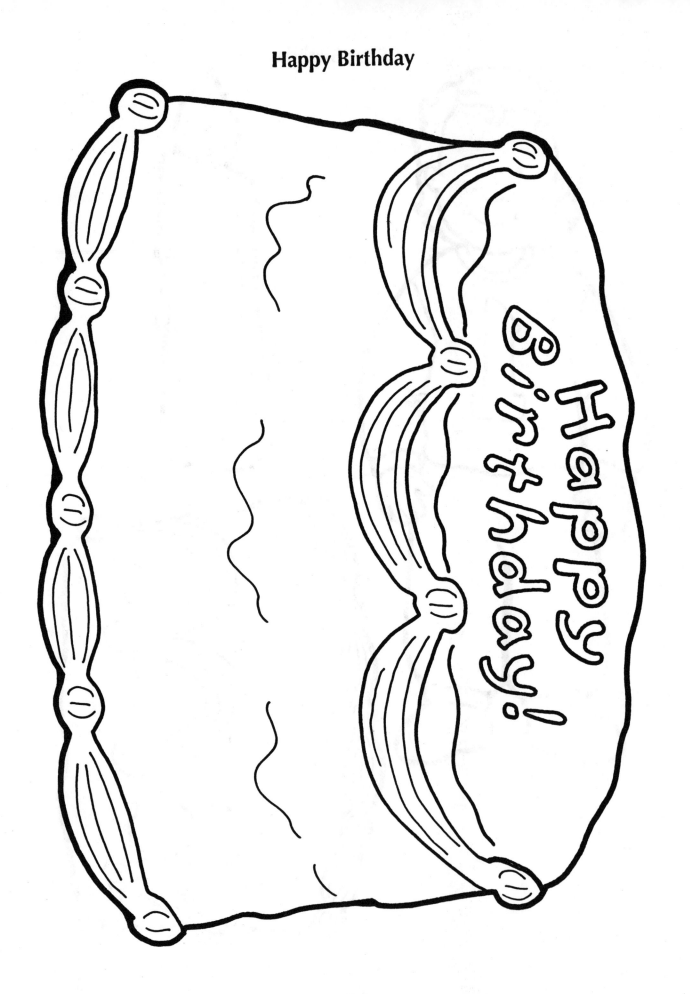

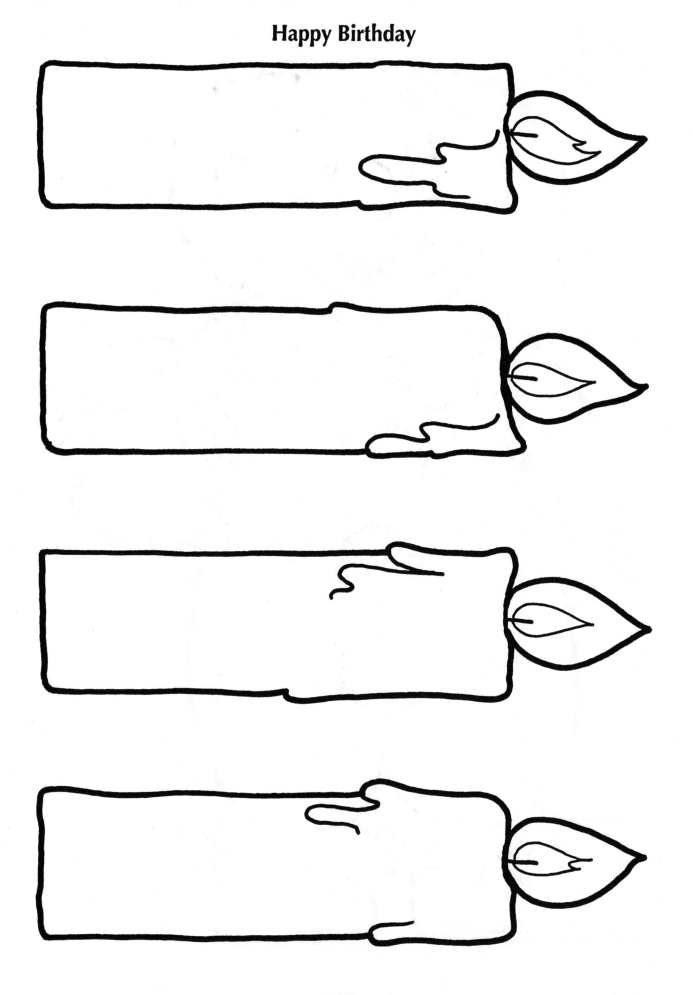

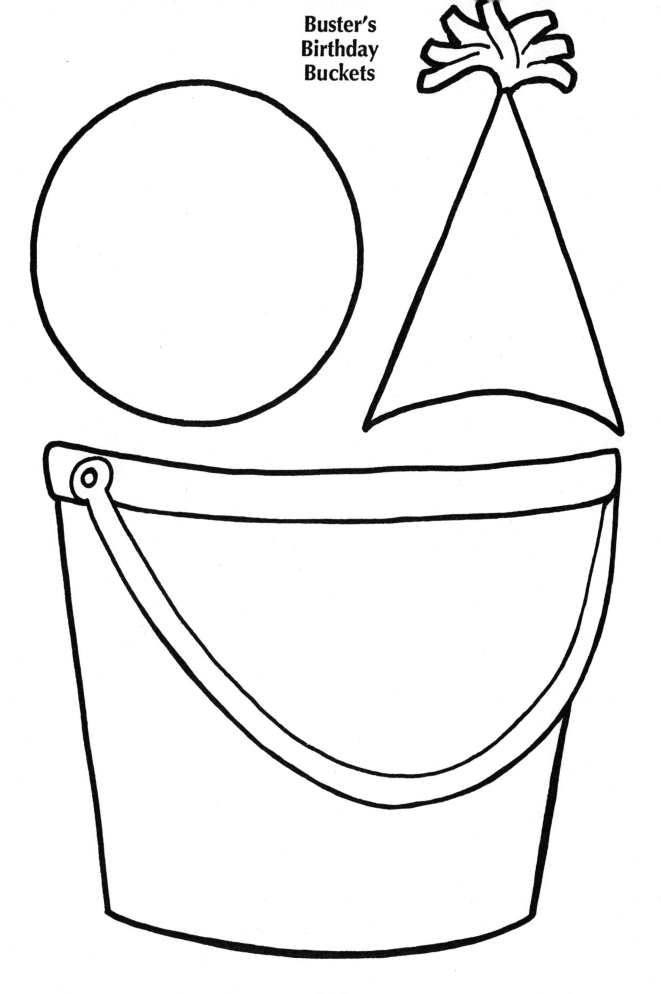

# FEELINGS

## MAKE

Use the feeling faces from the activity IF YOU'RE HAPPY AND YOU KNOW IT

## PEEK-A-BOO

Lay the feeling faces upside down on the floor. Have the children cover their eyes. Put a face on the felt board and slowly say:

*Peek-a-boo.*
*Is this you?*

Have the children uncover their eyes, look at the felt board, and make their faces look like the one on the board. Take the face off the board. Have the children cover their eyes again, while you display another feeling face and repeat the rhyme. Continue with the other faces, remembering to occasionally repeat ones you've already put up.

# FEELINGS

## MAKE

Feeling faces
  Happy
  Sad
  Mad
  Surprised
  Sleepy
  Sick

## IF YOU'RE HAPPY AND YOU KNOW IT

Tuck all of the feeling faces under your leg. Put the happy face on the felt board and begin singing, IF YOU'RE HAPPY AND YOU KNOW IT. After the first verse put another face on the board and continue singing. Keep going until you've sung about all of the faces.

IF YOU'RE HAPPY AND YOU KNOW IT
If you're happy and you know it clap your hands.
If you're happy and you know it clap your hands.
If you're happy and you know it
  then your face will really show it.
If you're happy and you know it clap your hands.

If you're sad and you know it keep on crying.
If you're sad and you know it keep on crying.
If you're sad and you know it
  then your face will really show it.
If you're sad and you know it keep on crying.

If you're mad and you know it give a frown.
If you're mad and you know it give a frown.
If you're mad and you know it
  then your face will really show it.
If you're mad and you know it give a frown.

If you're surprised and you know it open your mouth.
If you're surprised and you know it open your mouth.
If you're surprised and you know it
  then your face will really show it.
If you're surprised and you know it open your mouth.

If you're sleepy and you know it give a yawn.
If you're sleepy and you know it give a yawn.
If you're sleepy and you know it
  then your face will really show it.
If you're sleepy and you know it give a yawn.

If you're sick and you know it cough and sneeze.
If you're sick and you know it cough and sneeze.
If you're sick and you know it
  then your face will really show it.
If you're sick and you know it cough and sneeze.

# FEELINGS

## MAKE

Happy child
Sad child

## HAPPY OR SAD

Put the happy and sad child on the felt board. Tell your children a very short story about a happy or sad child. After the story have your children pretend to be the child in the story and make a happy or sad face. As they are making the face, point to the matching felt child.

Here are several stories to get you started:

• *Carin wants to wear the firefighter's hat. She goes over to the shelf, finds it, and puts it on her head. She walks over to the mirror and looks at herself. Does she feel happy or sad when she looks in the mirror?* (Make the face.)

• *It is Cathy's birthday. Her mom makes her favorite cake — a chocolate one with white frosting. How do your think Cathy feels when she sees it?* (Make the face.)

• *Greg is riding in his fire engine. He turns the corner too fast and tips over. Greg falls out and starts to cry. Is Greg feeling happy or sad?*

• *Eric painted a picture at school. He took it home and gave it to his mom. She smiled at him. Does Eric feel happy or sad that his mom liked his painting?*

• *Shel is blowing lots of bubbles into the air and then chasing them all over the playground. Does Shel feel happy or sad to play with bubbles?*

# FEELINGS

## MAKE

Snail

Ant

Whale

Basset

Lark

Bunny

Shark

Toad

Fox

Kitten

Ox

Lion

Clam

Rhino

Lamb

Tiger

Shrimp

Poodle

Chimp

Lizard

Bee

## PROPS

QUICK AS A
CRICKET book
or a copy of the
STORY CARD

## QUICK AS A CRICKET, Story Card

Duplicate the STORY CARD, glue it to a piece of construction paper, and laminate or cover it with clear adhesive paper. Have all of the felt animals in order tucked under your legs.

Start saying each line of the story. As you do, put up the animals and let the children call out what it is.

# QUICK AS A CRICKET

## Audrey Wood

The story begins, "I'm slow as a snail."

The story continues: ".... small as an ant."

".... large as a whale."

".... sad as a basset."

".... happy as a lark."

".... nice as a bunny."

".... mean as a shark."

".... cold as a toad."

".... hot as a fox."

".... weak as a kitten."

".... strong as an ox."

".... loud as a lion."

".... quiet as a clam."

".... tough as a rhino."

".... gentle as a lamb."

".... brave as a tiger."

".... shy as a shrimp."

".... tame as a poodle."

".... wild as a chimp."

".... lazy as a lizard."

".... busy as a bee."

"Put it all together,
It's ME!"

168

# Happy or Sad

# Quick As a Cricket

# Quick As a
# Cricket

Quick As a
Cricket

# SHAPES

## MAKE

Circle
Square
Triangle
Rectangle

## PEEK-A-BOO SHAPES

Put the circle, triangle, rectangle, and square on the felt board. Point to each one and have all the children call out its name.

Take the shapes off the board and tuck them under your leg. Have the children cover their eyes. Put one shape on the board and say,

*Peek-a-boo*
*A shape for you.*

Let the children uncover their eyes while you're pointing at the shape. You and the children call out what it is. You repeat the name of the shape while tracing around the edge of it with your finger. Everyone clap.

Take the shape off the board and have the children cover their eyes again. Put another shape on the board and play again. Continue playing using the shapes again and again.

VARIATION: Instead of using the large shapes use a set of tiny or small shapes. (Use patterns from other activities.)

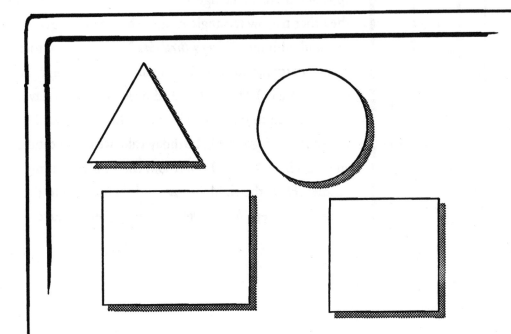

# SHAPES

## MAKE

5"x7" white rectangle

7" pink circle

2, 11/2"x6" rectangles
(skin tones)

2, small orange triangles

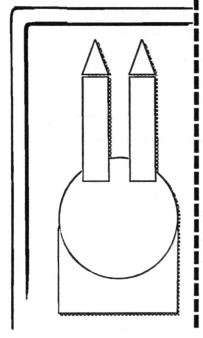

## SHAPE STORIES

There are two SHAPE STORIES, _The Birthday Cake_ and _Snowball Friends._ When telling your children these stories, use the felt pieces to develop a significant object for the story. At the end, let the children guess what it is.

## THE BIRTHDAY CAKE

Put all of the felt pieces behind the felt board.

I am so excited, because today is my birthday and I am two years old. I am going to have a birthday party. My friend Greg and his mom are coming over to my house. (Put white rectangle on the board.) As they are walking up to my door, I notice that Greg is carrying a big, round present, wrapped in pink paper. (Put the pink circle over the upper half of the white rectangle.) When they knock, I run to let them in. Greg (put one narrow rectangle over the circle) and his mom (put the other narrow rectangle next to the first one) give me a big hug and wish me, _"Happy Birthday."_ I give each of them an orange party hat to wear. (Put small orange triangles at top of each rectangle.) Then we walked over to my birthday table. What do you think we saw in the middle of the table? (Guess.) Yes, a great, big birthday cake with two candles. We all sang HAPPY BIRTHDAY and then I blew out my candles. Have the children sing and then blow out the candles. As they _"blow"_ take the candles off the cake.

# SHAPES

## MAKE

6" white circle
41/2" white circle
31/2" white circle
Black top hat

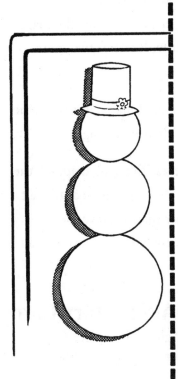

## SNOWBALL FRIENDS

Put all three snowballs in the upper left-hand corner of the felt board and the top hat tucked under your leg. In the story three snowballs roll down a hill. As you are rolling the felt snowballs down the hill, have your children roll their arms and chant, *"roll, roll, roll, roll..."* until each snowball has reached the bottom.

Once upon a time there were three snowball friends who decided to roll down the big snow hill. The largest one said, *"I'm the biggest so I'll go first and meet you two at the bottom."* (Roll the largest circle in a diagonal from the top corner of the board to the bottom. Have the children roll their arms and chant.)

Then the middle-size snowball shouted, *"Here I come!"* as she started rolling down the hill. (Roll the middle-sized snowball. Have the children roll their arms and chant.) When she got to the bottom, she bumped into the largest snowball and said, *"Hi friend"* as she climbed onto the biggest one's shoulders. (Set the middle-sized snowball on the largest one.)

The two snowball friends shouted to the smallest one, *"Come on down, it's fun"* so the smallest snowball started rolling down the hill. (Roll the small snowball. Have the children roll their arms and chant.) Soon he banged into his friends. He was so excited to see them that he jumped up onto his large friend and then climbed onto his middle-sized friend's shoulders. (Move the small snowball to the top as you talk.)

*"It is really high up here. I can see inside this window.* (Put the top hat on top of the smallest snowball.) *You know what's going on in there? Two children are getting ready to come outside and play in the snow. Who do you think they'll see as soon as they walk outside?"*

# SHAPES

## MAKE

Large, different-
    colored shapes:
        Squares
        Circles
        Triangles
Small, different-
    colored shapes:
        Squares
        Circles
        Triangles

## MAKE

Use the large
    square, circle,
    and triangle from
    the activity
    SHOUT FOR
    SHAPES.

## PROP

Same size and color
    construction
    paper square,
    circle, and
    triangle for each
    child

## MAKE

SPOT
Circle, Square
Diamond
Rectangle, Star
Triangle, Oval

## SHOUT FOR SHAPES

Set all the large squares behind the felt board. Quietly pick up one square, such as the red one, and say to the children, *"Watch carefully. I'm putting a 'red square' on the felt board. Let's shout for the 'red' square'."* (Put the shape on the board and everyone call out *"red square."* Clap.) Take that shape off the board and play again — and again — and again.

## WHICH ONE IS MISSING?

Have the felt circle, square, and triangle behind the felt board. Have the construction paper shapes nearby. Put one felt shape on the felt board , name it, and then give each child a matching construction paper shape. Name the shape as you give it to each child. Repeat with one or two more shapes.

Point to each shape on the felt board, name it, and let the children echo it back and hold up their matching shapes.

Have the children cover their eyes. Take one shape off the board. Have the children uncover their eyes, look at the felt shapes and their construction paper shapes. Have the children hold up the shape that is missing and everyone call out its name. Play again.

## SPOT LOOKS AT SHAPES, Story Card

Duplicate the STORY CARD, glue it to a piece of construction paper, and laminate or cover it with clear adhesive paper.

Put each shape on the felt board as you tell the children what Spot the dog is doing.

# SPOT LOOKS AT SHAPES

## Eric Hill

The story begins,

> "Spot's rubber ring is a round shape."

The story continues:

Drawing a bird on square paper.

Flying a kite.

Putting a rectangle flag in his sand castle.

Looking at a starfish in the sand.

Playing a triangle instrument.

Fishing in a oval pond.

At the end, point to and name all of the shapes.

**Peek-A-Boo Shapes**

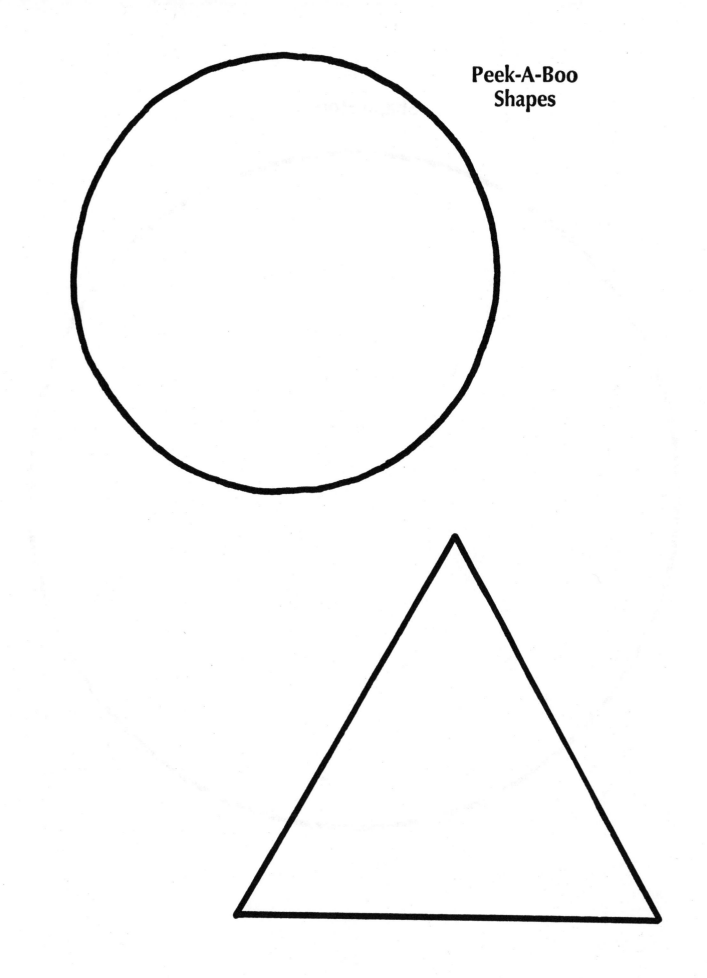

**Peek-A-Boo
Shapes**

# Shape Stories

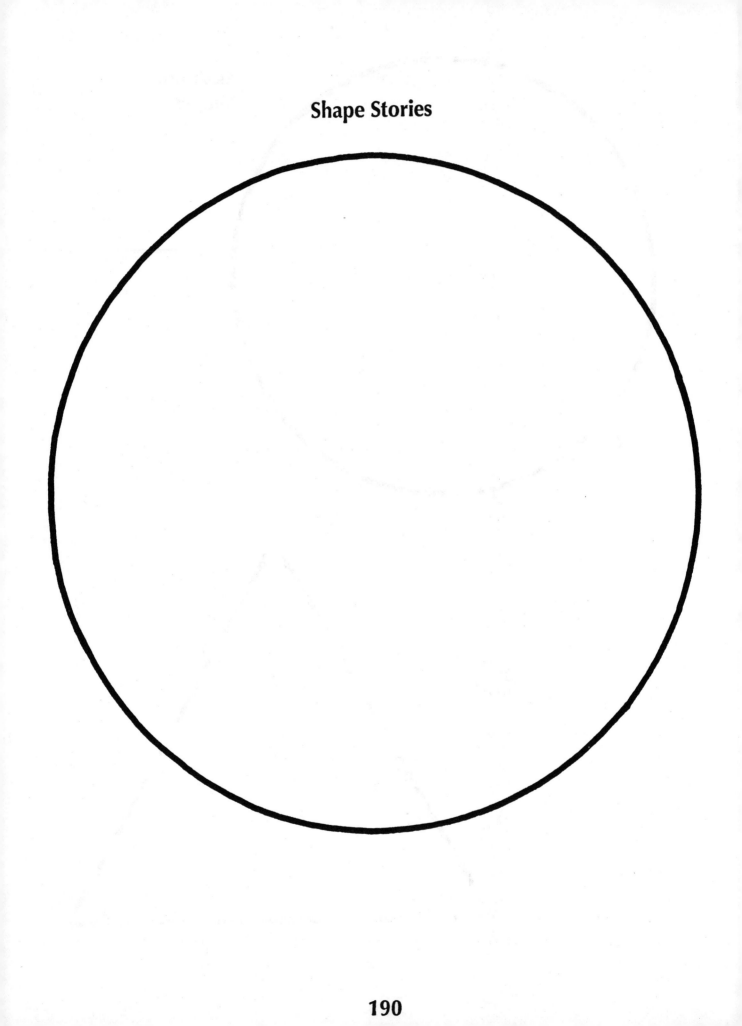

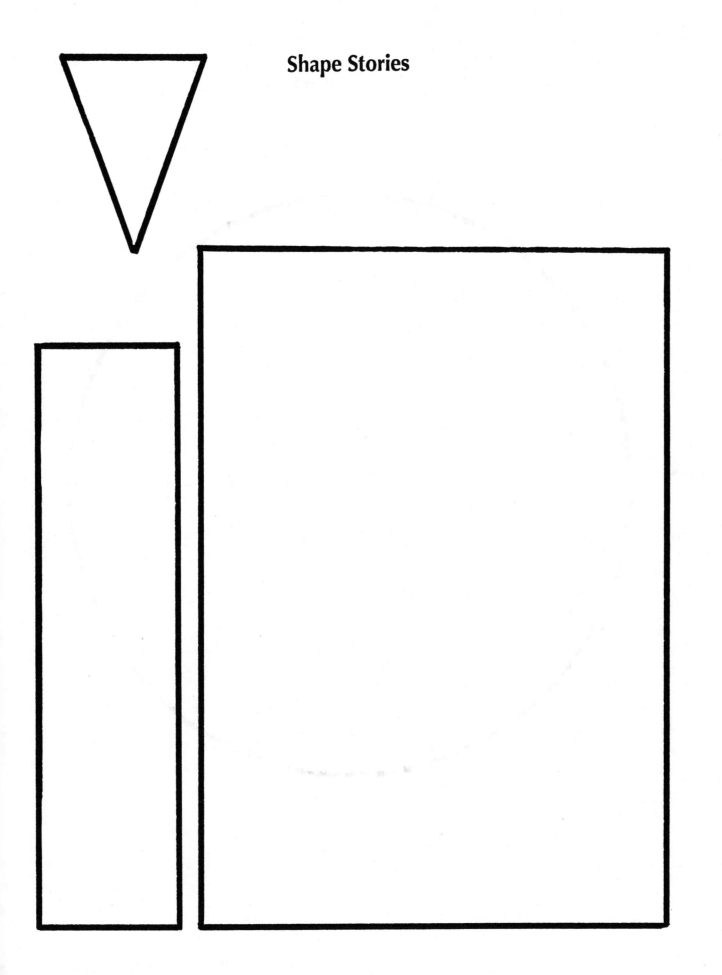

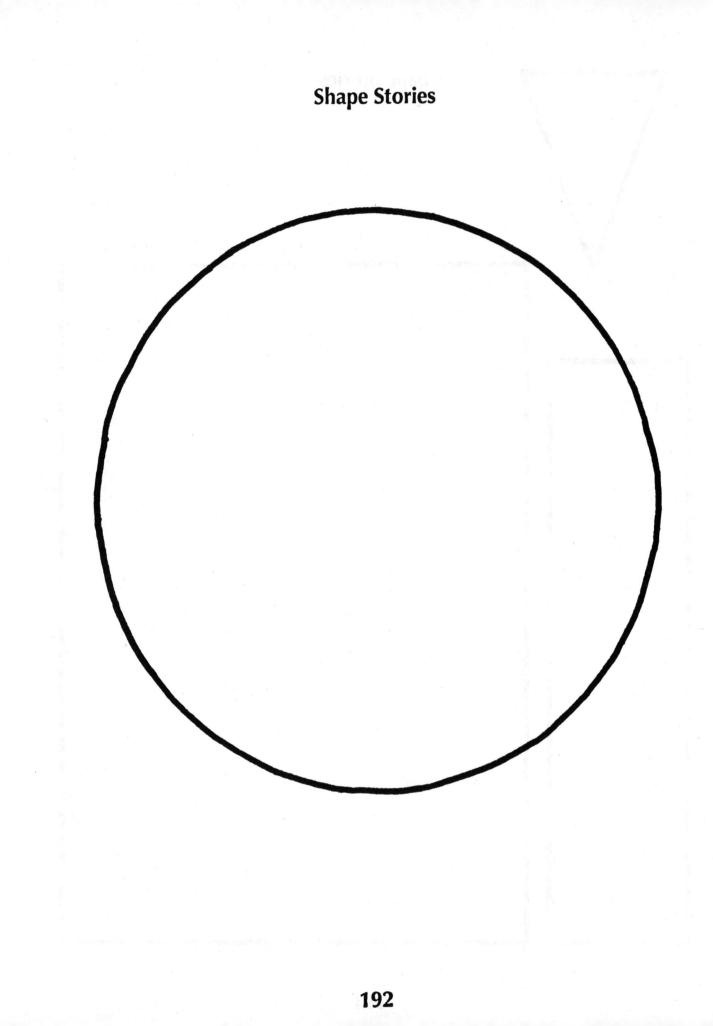

# Shape Stories

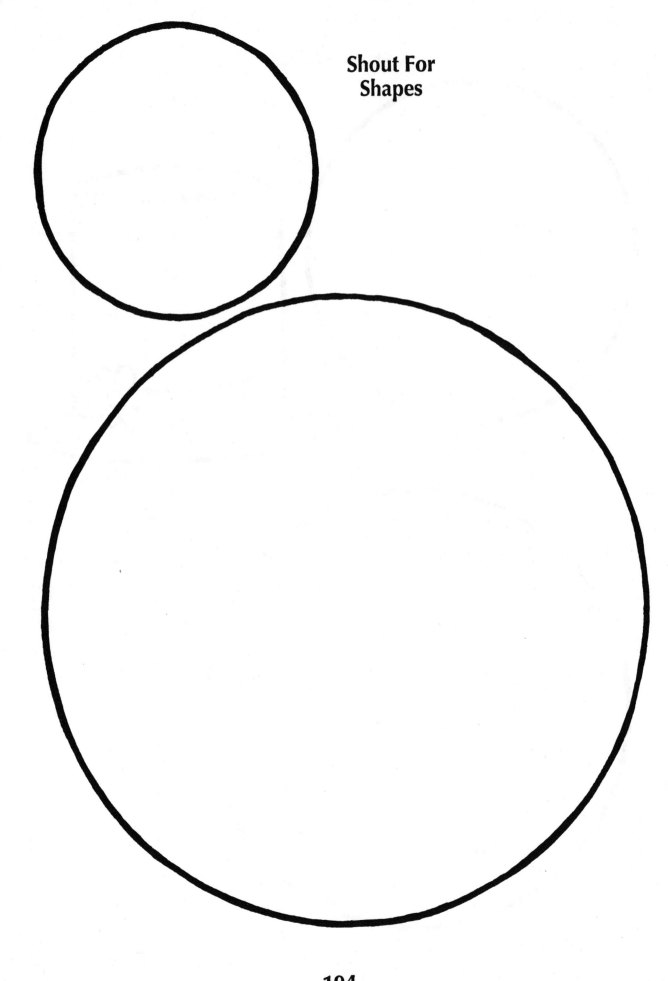

**Shout For
Shapes**

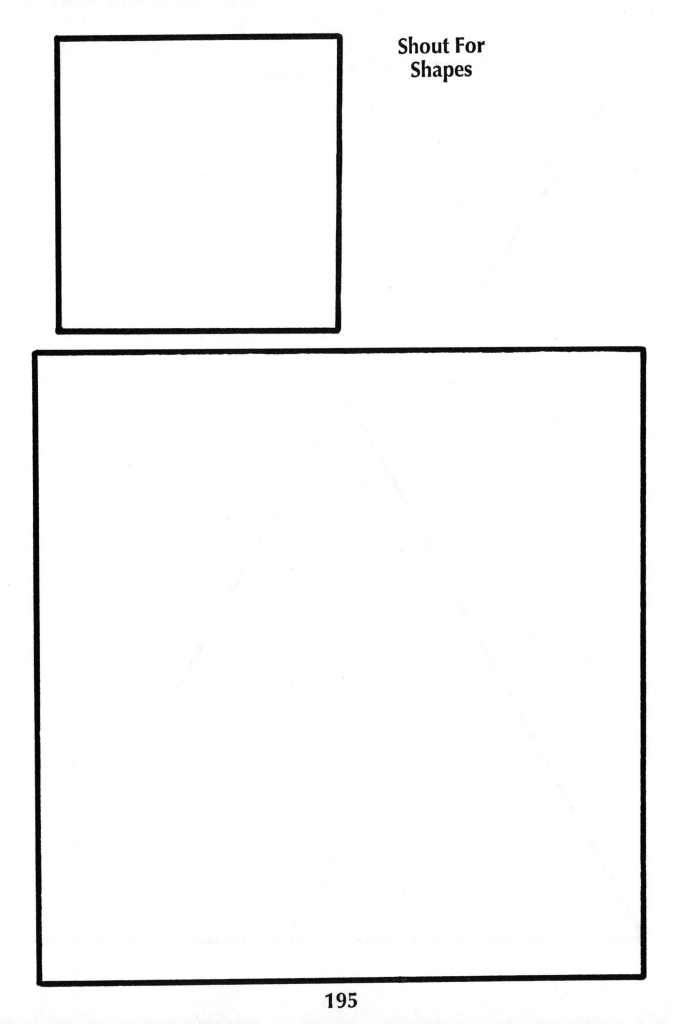

**Shout For
Shapes**

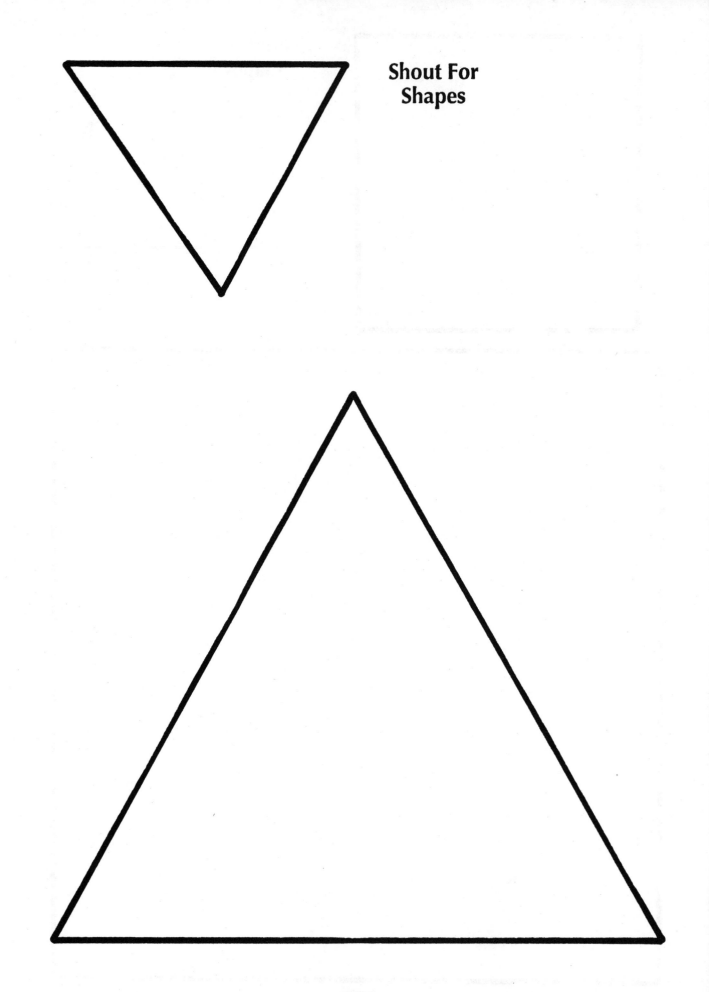

**Shout For
Shapes**

# Spot Looks At Shapes

# Library

## The Circle Time Series

*by Liz and Dick Wilmes.* Hundreds of activities for large and small groups of children. Each book is filled with Language and Active games, Fingerplays, Songs, Stories, Snacks, and more. A great resource for every library shelf.

### Circle Time Book
Captures the spirit of 39 holidays and seasons.
**ISBN 0-943452-00-7**                    **$ 12.95**

### Everyday Circle Times
Over 900 ideas. Choose from 48 topics divided into 7 sections: self-concept, basic concepts, animals, foods, science, occupations, and recreation.
**ISBN 0-943452-01-5**                    **$16.95**

### More Everyday Circle Times
Divided into the same 7 sections as EVERYDAY. Features new topics such as Birds and Pizza, plus all new ideas for some popular topics contained in EVERYDAY.
**ISBN 0-943452-14-7**                    **$16.95**

### Yearful of Circle Times
52 different topics to use weekly, by seasons, or mixed throughout the year. New Friends, Signs of Fall, Snowfolk Fun, and much more.
**ISBN 0-943452-10-4**                    **$16.95**

## Paint Without Brushes

*by Liz and Dick Wilmes.* Use common materials which you already have. Discover the painting possibilities in your classroom! PAINT WITHOUT BRUSHES gives your children open-ended art activities to explore paint in lots of creative ways. A valuable art resource. One you'll want to use daily.
**ISBN 0-943452-15-5**                    **$12.95**

## Easel Art

*by Liz & Dick Wilmes.* Let the children use easels, walls, outside fences, clip boards, and more as they enjoy the variety of art activities filling the pages of EASEL ART. A great book to expand young children's art experiences.
**ISBN 0-943452-25-2**                    **$ 12.95**

## Everyday Bulletin Boards

*by Wilmes and Moehling.* Features borders, murals, backgrounds, and other open-ended art to display on your bulletin boards. Plus board ideas with patterns, which teachers can make and use to enhance their curriculum.
**ISBN 0-943452-09-0**                    **$ 12.95**

## Exploring Art

*by Liz and Dick Wilmes.* EXPLORING ART is divided by months. Over 250 art ideas for paint, chalk, doughs, scissors, and more. Easy to set-up in your classroom.
**ISBN 0-943452-05-8**                    **$19.95**

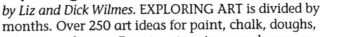
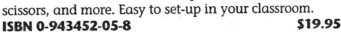

### Parachute Play

*by Liz and Dick Wilmes.* A year 'round approach to one of the most versatile pieces of large muscle equipment. Starting with basic techniques, PARACHUTE PLAY provides over 100 activities to use with your parachute.
**ISBN 0-943452-03-1**                    **$ 9.95**

### Learning Centers

*by Liz and Dick Wilmes.* Hundreds of open-ended activities to quickly involve and excite your children. You'll use it every time you plan and whenever you need a quick, additional activity. A must for every teacher's bookshelf.
**ISBN 0-943452-13-9**                    **$19.95**

### Play With Big Boxes

*by Liz and Dick Wilmes.* Children love big boxes. Turn them into boats, telephone booths, tents, and other play areas. Bring them to art and let children collage, build, and paint them. Use them in learning centers for games, walk-along vehicles, play stages, quiet spaces, puzzles, and more, more, more.
**ISBN 0-943452-23-6**                    **$ 12.95**

### Play With Small Boxes

*by Liz and Dick Wilmes.* Small boxes are free, fun, and provide unlimited possibilities. Use them for telephones, skates, scoops, pails, beds, buggies, and more. So many easy activities, you'll want to use small boxes every day.
**ISBN 0-943452-24-4**                    **$ 12.95**

### Felt Board Fingerplays

*by Liz and Dick Wilmes.* Over fifty popular fingerplays, each with full-size patterns. All accompanied by games and activities to extend the learning and play even more. Divided by seasons, this book is a quick reference for a year full of fingerplay fun.
**ISBN 0-943452-26-0**                    **$16.95**

### Felt Board Fun

*by Liz and Dick Wilmes.* Make your felt board come alive. Discover how versatile it is as the children become involved with a wide range of activities. This unique book has over 150 ideas with accompanying patterns.
**ISBN 0-943452-02-3**                    **$16.95**

### Table & Floor Games

*by Liz and Dick Wilmes.* 32 easy-to-make, fun-to-play table/floor games with accompanying patterns ready to trace or photocopy. Teach beginning concepts such as matching, counting, colors, alphabet, sorting and so on.
**ISBN 0-943452-16-3**                    **$19.95**

### Activities Unlimited

*by Adler, Caton, and Cleveland.* Create an enthusiasm for learning! Hundreds of innovative activities to help your children develop fine and gross motor skills, increase their language, become self-reliant, and play cooperatively. Whether you're a beginning teacher or a veteran, this book will quickly become one of your favorites.
**ISBN 0-943452-17-1**                    **$16.95**

# 2's Experience Series

*by Liz and Dick Wilmes.* An exciting series developed especially for toddlers and twos!

## 2's Experience - Art
Scribble, Paint, Smear, Mix, Tear, Mold, Taste, and more. Over 150 activities, plus lots of recipes and hints.
**ISBN 0-943452-21-X**                    **$16.95**

## 2's Experience - Dramatic Play
Dress up and pretend! Hundreds of imaginary characters... fire-fighters, campers, bus drivers, and more.
**ISBN 0-943452-20-1**                    **$12.95**

## 2's Experience - Felt Board Fun
Make your felt board come alive. Enjoy stories, activities, and rhymes developed just for very young children. Hundreds of extra large patterns feature teddy bears, birthdays, farm animals, and much, much more.
**ISBN 0-943452-19-8**                    **$14.95**

## 2's Experience - Fingerplays
A wonderful collection of easy fingerplays with accompanying games and large FINGERPLAY CARDS.
**ISBN 0-943452-18-X**                    **$12.95**

## 2's Experience - Sensory Play
Hundreds of playful, multi-sensory activities to encourage children to look, listen, taste, touch, and smell.
**ISBN 0-943452-22-8**                    **$14.95**

**T O D D L E R S   &   T W O ' S**

| | |
|---|---|
| **BUILDING BLOCKS Subscription** | **$20.00** |
| **2's EXPERIENCE Series** | |
| 2'S EXPERIENCE - ART | 16.95 |
| 2'S EXPERIENCE - DRAMATIC PLAY | 12.95 |
| 2'S EXPERIENCE - FELTBOARD FUN | 14.95 |
| 2'S EXPERIENCE - FINGERPLAYS | 12.95 |
| 2'S EXPERIENCE - SENSORY PLAY | 14.95 |
| **CIRCLE TIME Series** | |
| CIRCLE TIME BOOK | 12.95 |
| EVERYDAY CIRCLE TIMES | 16.95 |
| MORE EVERYDAY CIRCLE TIMES | 16.95 |
| YEARFUL OF CIRCLE TIMES | 16.95 |
| **ART** | |
| EASEL ART | 12.95 |
| EVERYDAY BULLETIN BOARDS | 12.95 |
| EXPLORING ART | 19.95 |
| PAINT WITHOUT BRUSHES | 12.95 |
| **LEARNING GAMES & ACTIVITIES** | |
| ACTIVITIES UNLIMITED | 16.95 |
| FELT BOARD FINGERPLAYS | 16.95 |
| FELT BOARD FUN | 16.95 |
| LEARNING CENTERS | 19.95 |
| PARACHUTE PLAY | 9.95 |
| PLAY WITH BIG BOXES | 12.95 |
| PLAY WITH SMALL BOXES | 12.95 |
| TABLE & FLOOR GAMES | 19.95 |

Prices subject to change without notice.

*All books available from full-service book stores, educational stores, and school supply catalogs.*